Anonymous

Christ is coming! : Part I.

Evidences of the existence of God

Anonymous

Christ is coming! : Part I.
Evidences of the existence of God

ISBN/EAN: 9783337283957

Printed in Europe, USA, Canada, Australia, Japan

Cover: Foto ©Lupo / pixelio.de

More available books at **www.hansebooks.com**

"The Boils on the Souls of Men have come to a Head—lance them."

CHRIST IS COMING!

Part I.—EVIDENCES OF THE EXISTENCE OF GOD, AND OF THE TRUTH OF THE HOLY SCRIPTURES.
Published March 2nd, 1868.

Parts II. & III.—THE HOLY SCRIPTURES AND THEIR DESCRIPTION OF THE MIGHTY PLAN OF GOD.
Published September 1st, 1868.

Parts IV. & V.—THE HOLY TEACHINGS OF GOD, AND THE RE-ORGANIZATION OF THE ONE HOLY UNIVERSAL CHURCH OF CHRIST.
Published September, 1869.

Part VI.—CHRIST THE GLORIOUS KING OVER THE WHOLE EARTH.
Will be published, September, 1874.

PARTS I., II., III., IV., & V.

"Let every Man, every Woman, and every Child be quick and spread around the glorious news that Christ is Coming."

FOURTH EDITION.—PRICE ONE SHILLING AND SIXPENCE.

LONDON:
PRINTED AND PUBLISHED FOR THE AUTHOR BY
JOHN B. DAY, 3, SAVOY STREET, STRAND,
AND TO BE HAD OF ALL BOOKSELLERS IN TOWN AND COUNTRY.

1871.

CHRIST IS COMING.

PART I.

EVIDENCES OF THE EXISTENCE OF GOD,

AND OF THE

TRUTH OF THE HOLY SCRIPTURES.

TO THE NATIONS.

IN the name of the Mighty God, the creator of all things, to you, oh ye Nations of the whole earth! these words are sent. Into your hearts let them be deeply engraven; and do ye ponder over them; for, like as seed that falls upon fruitful ground bears fruit in plenty, so will these words bear plenteous fruit among the nations of the world. Now, oh ye nations! ye are as wild sheep, scattered and isolated, but hereafter ye shall all form *one* flock under *one* Shepherd.

THE ever-living God, the creator of the starry skies, and of all things—Who is as invisible to the eyes of man as the air we breathe, and Who, although invisible to us, is like the air, near to and surrounding every one of us, has given to man free will;

and having given to man His Holy Scriptures, as man's only true guide, has left to man the duty of working out his own salvation. God looks upon all mankind as *one* earthly family, and holds each one responsible for the misdeeds of the rest. Therefore, God permits evil men to afflict the good;—for the good fall short of their duty to their fellow-men in permitting them to grow up in ignorance of God, in permitting hazy notions of God to exist among men, and in permitting evil men to exercise the power of the nations.

Mankind, from the days of Adam, have perverted that holy thing, the soul, which gives them their intelligence; from being spirits of good, they have become spirits of mischief; instead of being angels of earth, they have become the evil spirits of the earth; using the intelligence of their souls in devising all manner of mischief against their own kind; studying their own individual inclinations, and forgetful of God. Verily, mankind have dishonoured themselves more than any beast of the ground, or bird of the air, or fish of the waters. The iron intended for the ploughshare, cruel man has shaped into the murdering sword, the murdering tube, and the murdering bullet, wherewith to slay his own kind, and for sport, the other living creatures of the earth. They have departed widely from the precepts of God, and happiness has fled from the earth; and men have become, as it were, mere beasts of burden, less joyous and less contented than the free creatures of the ground, of the air, and of the waters. Mankind have adulterated the Word of God by adding their own foolish theories to its wisdom; and men have so taught their sons and daughters that they have become as foolish as themselves. To the worship of God and of His Glorious Son many foolish ones have added the worship of images, of reputed saints, and of a supposed Queen of Heaven, and have thereby brought the Word of God into disrepute,—perpetuating misery throughout the earth.

Verily the minds of men have been filled with nonsense, and their nonsense has whipped the nations, as it were, with whips of knotted cord. When distress covers thee, oh nations !— when the people are perplexed, and hungry, and naked—when the nations are warring one against the other—and when the ambitious and the unjust man, the adulterer, the fornicator, the thief, and the murderer, take up their abode with thee, and are suffered to teach thy people all manner of mischief, and sorely oppressing them,—it is not God who brings these evils upon mankind, they are the natural offspring of wickedness—of wickedness of the nations. In like manner, oh man! if thou wert violently to dash thyself against a stone, pain will be the natural offspring of the act; so, when the nations dash themselves against the precepts of God, as declared in the Holy Scriptures, misery and pain to themselves necessarily follow.

Those who overrule thee, oh nations! are unwise; they teach thee folly; their laws are foolish, and they administer the laws foolishly; they have placed before thee the foolish maxims of men, and God is almost ignored: therefore God for thy folly has permitted mankind to have their way. Thou hast taken into thy bosom, as it were, cruel scorpions, and they sting and pain thee. Behold your folly! Nation is arrayed against nation—the one to make miserable the other. Their desire is to destroy each other for ever; and for what? As dogs they snarl, as dogs they fight, and as dogs they reap bloodthirstiness, and violence, and duplicity, and wretchedness, and hate; and as fighting dogs they die. Ye foolish nations! ye have placed yourselves under the rule of murderers, through your disunion, and they give you justice that is perverted into robbery, into lies, into duplicity, into violence; safety, that is destruction; rest, that is feverish anxiety and poverty; and they give you for ministers of God, men as perverted and corrupt as yourselves.

Oh, foolish nations! following like silly sheep the foolish antics of a few of thy people not a whit wiser than yourselves; poor nations! thou art saturated with folly and with misery, because the spurious wisdom of the wicked ones which has ruled thy fathers, and which still rules thee, appears fair to thee—for long continued wickedness has blinded the people, and common sense has become uncommon ; but within all is rottenness, all is pretence, all is sham. Oh! that this wicked generation would quickly learn to understand that it is far better to be at peace than to be at war—to love each other than to hate—to be filled with holy rest than filled with anxiety; and learn to understand that it is far better to obey God than to live in forgetfulness of Him; to be united together as one holy Christian family of men, than be separated into nations—as it were one of dogs, another of foxes, another of wolves, and another of tigers—living like them, and dying like them.

Learn, oh ye nations! and understand, that when thy kind increased in their hate one for the other, and the more mutual love departed from their hearts, then the more did the Holy Spirit of God—which, like the invisible air is near to every one of us—shrink from those nations, for their wickedness was abhorent to God ; then did the partial withdrawal of God cause partial disruption, and the air, and the water, and the ground, became corrupt, and pestilence and famine, and earthquakes and great storms, and misery accompanied their hate and their disobedience.

Now consider, oh ye nations of the world! Let these words sink deeply into your hearts. Have ye as little understanding as dogs? Have ye as little love for the more peaceful nations as cruel wolves have for the peaceful sheep? Ye have truly that holy thing, the soul, but ye appear to know it not, because ye play the part of the senseless brutes ; for, as senseless wolves ye slay your own kind maliciously, and outstrip them in glorying in it. Oh foolish nations,—mutual tormenters! learn that the nation which incites to war, and that is the aggressor, fights against God, and God has ever punished that nation, and henceforth will punish it more intensely. Be wise, sternly turn from your councils and from their thrones, the chief inciters to bloodshed; let their names be branded as murderers of their kind, and drive them from your nation, and let their wives, and their sons and daughters be also outcasts. For it is better sternly to disown a few, than to suffer them to stir up hate between the nations. Be wise, ye nations, and settle amicably your differences, with honesty avoiding all duplicity.

Up now, ye foolish nations! hasten thee, tear off the bandage folly has placed round thine eyes, and learn true wisdom—the wisdom of God, which excelleth the wisdom of man far more than the sun excels in brightness the flickering candle. Behold the time is close at hand, even knocking at the door, when God will remove the scales from your mental eyes, and ye shall behold Him and His glorious Son, our Redeemer, as they are. And the paths of earthly happiness, and the paths to Heaven shall be as well laid roads, hedged on either side, that ye may no longer go astray, but be wise, walking with a firm tread, understanding God and His holy teachings. Think not, oh nations! that the paths your God wishes you to tread are paths of sorrow. *Your* paths are joyless, full of anxiety, and full of fear; but His paths are full of contentment, of holy peace, of serene joy, and as it were, in the midst of beauteous sweet-smelling flowers. Let every man therefore be honest and tender-hearted, mindful of the necessities of his fellow men, resolutely resisting all temptation to do or think evil, remembering always that man's earthly happiness is bound up with that of his fellow men, as though he and they formed the body of one man, so that if one member suffers, all suffer.

Does God expect thee, oh generation of evil men, to turn your disobedient hearts to him? No; for well He knows how greatly your understanding has been perverted, and your unwillingness to learn aright; but your children will learn of Him; yet more their children; and still more their children's children; so that love between man and man will abound, and the Holy Spirit of God will enter the earth as in the early days of Adam, and it will become once more holy in His sight. But not yet, for the nations are swayed by the false and selfish maxims of men, and have ignored the wise maxims of God; swayed by the foolish notions of philosophers—of philosophers lost in vanity and infidelity—which notions, belonging wholly to the imaginations of men, are full of nonsense, and bewilder and lead astray from the true path, the thoughtless among mankind. Ye philosophers, leaders of the people! ye wise in your own conceit, and in the opinion of the foolish, because ye appear less foolish than themselves! ye forget that the little morality ye teach proceeded through the holy men of God in ancient time. Have ye traced out God in the wonders of Creation, in the wonders that surround you on every side? Have ye not rather wilfully stopped far short and promulgated theories worthy only of the foolish brutes? Have ye not ignored God and become as fools? Poor philosophers, blind leaders of the people, what has your spurious wisdom done for your own happiness and the happiness of the world? Spurious because but little being founded upon truth, is nonsense as a whole. Poor philosophers, blind leaders of blind people, weep, for your day is passed, and the world will henceforth laugh at your folly, and your pretentiousness will be ridiculed. Weep on, ye blind philosophers, leaders of blind people, offspring of a world heretofore darkened by your predecessors as blind as yourselves,—for the light of God's wisdom will cause men to see your blindness and your pretentious folly. Weep on, and repent, and enlighten your minds with God's wisdom, and do your very utmost to wipe away the stains of unbelief! your folly has spotted the souls of men.

And ye who officiate in sanctuaries called after the name of the Lord, be not more dull of understanding than the people whom you profess to teach; learn and understand that it is better, far better, to touch their hearts with the pure Word of God than to deceive them with utter folly. Learn and understand that such deceivers as yourselves have been great curses of mankind, having led men astray. It was such as yourselves who introduced idolatry and spurious worship—who instigated the shedding of the blood of the prophets—the slaying of the Holy Christ and of His holy followers. It was such as yourselves who countenanced war and bloodshed, and who perpetuated folly, disunion, and hatred among mankind. The people are eager for true spiritual light, and behold! your perverted understanding persists in misconstruing the Holy Scriptures, bewildering the people so that superstition has taken the place of common sense, and a jumble of a little truth and much nonsense is instilled into their youthful minds as the wisdom of God,—whereas it is but the foolish nonsense of your predecessors. God has provided for them the true spiritual Bread of Life, and lo! you, misguided teachers, give them adulterated bread wherewith to feed their souls. As it is with you, so it has been with your predecessors—all have erred, all have blinded their understanding with the trashy thoughts of men, and are blind to true wisdom. Give place, ye miserable foolish leaders! stand aside! in your stead shall rise up teachers whose lips shall teach true wisdom, because the Word of God will guide them and be their only guide, and they shall lead mankind into the right path, and, like faithful shepherds, keep them in it.

And ye, true worshippers of God, ye greatly err by your disunion; ye have thereby become almost powerless among men. Henceforth there shall be but *one* Church—the one old Church of Christ. What! are ye not brethren? Do ye hate each other, yet worship the same God and account yourselves the ransomed children of the same Christ? Yes; the unholy thing is whispered in your ears,—the adopted children of Christ hate and war against each other, because foolish teachers perverted the understanding of their fathers and continue to pervert theirs, and have, by impure worship and hate, become almost as sinful as the children of the wicked one.

And ye, unwise people, who make to yourselves images and pictures representing God—bowing down and reverencing before them—learn to discriminate what is evil and what is not evil in this matter. It is not evil for a good purpose to represent aught that thine eyes can see or that thy fellow men have seen; but it is an evil thing to represent aught as representing God, and it is a very evil thing to bow down and make obeisance before them; and a still more evil thing to supplicate God intentionally before them. Thy foolish teachers have erred in teaching thee so to do. Henceforth cease this folly and let thy prayers be uttered towards Heaven, the dwelling-place of God, and God will hear thee; but God refuses thy prayers when uttered before thine abominable representations.

Now understand, oh ye nations! and let these words sink deeply into your souls.

God made this round earth and the starry skies for His greatly-beloved angel Christ, that Christ might found a mighty and a holy kingdom in Heaven, the subjects thereof being the redeemed children of the man Adam, whom God purposed to create. God created the sun, the starry skies, and this round earth, filling it with all necessary things, and then He created the first man Adam, giving him *one* soul, which should be subdivided among all his descendants, in like manner as a lump of gold may be divided into countless millions of atoms, each atom being as truly gold as the great lump. Adam disobeyed God, and thereby introduced the tremendous sin of disobedience towards God into the world. Therefore, God deemed him unholy and unfit to enter holy Heaven—both Adam and all the unborn people within him; and God condemned the *one* soul to be banished from Heaven for ever, as are the unholy brutes. But God, having foreknowledge of Adam's disobedience, had planned, before He made the starry skies, that His beloved angel Christ, the future King of men, should win His kingship by saving His future subjects; and God planned that Christ should successfully pass through the ordeal of living upon the earth as a perfectly righteous man—as righteous in the sight of God as are the holy angels; and, furthermore, God planned that the holy Christ should give the life of His flesh and blood, suffering death ignominiously, as an all-sufficient atonement, once and for ever, for their souls. And God ordained that all the souls of men who worshipped God, striving to obey His commandments, should thus be deemed ransomed, and be deemed holy and worthy to be His children and the adopted children and subjects of His Son Jesus Christ, the glorious Conqueror of sin—the King of Heaven. Thus did the righteous man Christ save many children of the unrighteous man Adam, and thus did the childless man Christ win many children by adoption.

Therefore, oh ye people! choose ye whether ye will be the adopted children and followers of the holy Christ, or unredeemed children of Satan—the disobedient man Adam.

Discern, oh ye nations! there are but two kinds of men, all descended from the man Adam.

The first kind are those who worship God, taking His Holy Scriptures as their guide.

The second kind are those who worship other gods; those who worship gods calling them the lesser name—saints; those who use images and pictures in their worship, and those who worship God with their lips, but have not the love of God in their hearts—disobeying Him.

The first are the redeemed ones of Christ, His adopted children and the children of His God and Father, the Almighty God our Creator; therefore they, being His adopted children, constitute His one Church upon earth and His future subjects in Heaven. These, oh ye Christian people of all lands, are thy brethren. Quickly band yourselves together, and let the love of God and of His glorious Son lead you to love and assist each other to the uttermost; be ye not slack nor rebellious, but prompt and obedient.

Now learn, oh ye Christians throughout the world! the appointed time of God is close at hand, even knocking at the door. Haste! put away your strife. Enlighten your understanding and purify yourselves by prayer,—for murderous wars shall cease, and the hearts of men will be softened, and they will look tenderly one upon the other, and their thoughts be heavenward—not tied to the things made by man, nor to the thoughts of men, but the Holy Spirit of God and of His glorious Son, present in the Holy Scriptures, shall in like manner be in their hearts; and the Word will no longer be as a sealed book to a perverted understanding, but plain to all men, for a right understanding will be given you, and you will be able, through a right knowledge of God, to resist easily the evil desires and inclinations of the body; and you shall forget the past wickedness of the world, and shall labour zealously and joyously in the world for the furtherance upon earth of the kingdom of your Lord and Saviour Jesus Christ. These things shall come to pass, but not fully come to pass—not until the fourth generation will the fruit be fully ripe.

Band yourselves quickly together, oh my Christian brothers! and you, oh my Christian sisters of every nation! hold up the Holy Scriptures as your guiding light, and disseminate its light, and this little explanatory book, around you on every side, at home and abroad; encourage those to the uttermost who strive after goodness; and discourage, to your very uttermost, those who follow evil; resolutely refuse to intermarry with them; neither suffer them to be placed in authority. In worldly matters you are energetic; be energetic now in the holy cause of your fellow-men and of God. Followers of God flock to the banner of Christ; for the final war is upon you, the mental war of the followers of good against the teachers of evil. Who shall doubt the result? for the Mighty God, who is the God of Abraham, of Isaac, of Jacob, and of our Lord Jesus Christ, is on our side. We are His children, His soldiers; therefore, with us will be the victory. We now commence the battle. You, my sisters, young and old—and you, my brothers, old and young—join in the fray, and be zealous, energetic soldiers of the Lord Christ. Let your arms be the Sword of the Spirit, which is the Word of God, and enlighten the understanding of the enemies of God, who will quickly become your friends; and, as fellow-soldiers, will assist you in your mental warfare with the evil that is running riot throughout the world: be energetic therefore, and persevere. And ye, faithful teachers of the Word of God, of every sect—ye blessed of the Father and of the Son—from your pulpits bring quickly to the notice of your flocks this little book, and urge them to ponder over it. And ye members of the press, in every nation, sound aloud the tocsin; loudly let the tocsin ring, shake up the sleepers, join quickly in the fray, and drive fables from the hearts of men. Publish in your papers, word by word, the contents of this little book, that the minds of all men may be quickly comforted, and that mutual love may drive away mutual hate for ever.

Let every man, every woman, and every child be quick, and spread around the glorious news that Christ is coming.

CHAPTER I.

The Difference between Man and all other Living Creatures.

MARK, oh man! how small is the intelligence of the most highly-trained of creeping things, of beasts of the earth, of fowls of the air, and of fishes of the waters, whose intelligence is about equal, compared with the most intelligent of thy fellow-men—those who worship God.

Understand, oh my brother! that of all living creatures man is born with least instinct—certain knowledge, which man calls instinct, being wondrously transmitted from one generation to another, each kind having its own peculiar knowledge at birth, as inherent to that kind as the shape of its body. Instinctively other living creatures do many things without thought, as thoughtlessly as a living tree pushes out its branches like other trees of its own kind—instinctively suckling, instinctively they seek out certain kinds of food, instinctively avoiding other food, instinctively know their own kind, not knowing their own shape; instinctively migrate, erring not; instinctively they build their nests, and the spider and the silkworm spin their webs; as their progenitors did, so, without thought, do they. But man is only born with the absolutely necessary instinct to suckle all other knowledge he afterwards becomes possessed of; he *acquires*—gaining knowledge vastly greater than any other living creature can possibly obtain. To man God has not given instinct; but instead thereof a soul, and perfect free-will—free to think, and free to act. Freedom which God has not given, for His wise purposes, to any other living creature.

Mark the great intelligence of man, how greatly it transcends that of every other living creature. Their knowledge is stationary. The instinct of the parents is transmitted intact to their offspring; whereas no knowledge that a man acquires does he transmit to his son, as he transmits the shape of his body.

Can any living creature, oh my brother! besides man, comprehend so as to worship God, or find out those laws of God which govern the things of this round earth, known as chemistry, mechanics, astronomy? Is any other living creature capable of building ships of various sizes, or machines of various forms; or able to read or write, or transmit knowledge through books or writings; or bring to light or mould into many shapes the serviceable metals; or cause the earth to bring forth fruit;—these things the most ignorant man may be taught, but not so the brutes.

Wherefore is it not possible? Some have greater bulk, greater strength, greater keenness of smell of sight and of hearing, than man; the constitution of their flesh and blood and bones, are quite equal to those of man. What thing then is it that makes the vast difference between man and every other living creature? What is it that stamps him, as his birthright, the *visible* Lord of all the living creatures, and of all the living vegetation of the earth? Does the horse obey the lion? Does the lion obey the horse? How numerous are the living creatures which obey man, or flee from him instinctively? Man causes those to multiply which are serviceable to him, and destroys those that are noxious to him; bending to his service the huge, the strong, and the small. He purposely sows seed, comprehending beforehand what will ensue, and behold the earth brings forth fruit and verdure as it were at his bidding, and as it were owning man for its *visible* lord. And upon the ocean he sails his numerous ships, bending even the seas to his service. What is it that gives to man his pre-eminence?

And behold, oh my brother! the beauty and strength of the brute creation—some more beauteous, and some stronger than any of thy kind, having bones and flesh and blood like as thou hast; nevertheless the most decrepit worshipper of God excels them vastly in thy sight, and in the sight of the great Creator of all things.

Again I ask thee, oh man! what thing is it that places, as it were, a vast gulf between intelligent man and every other living creature? Is it the size of the brain? No; for the elephant and the whale are not more intelligent than are minute living creatures, therefore difference in the size of the brain is not the cause? Is man more sensitive in his body than they? No; for living creatures are as sensitive to pleasure and pain as is man. What then, finally, is it that separates all other living creatures so widely from man? It is that unseen *living* thing that is in every one of us, and which men call the *soul*, without which men would be as brutish as the gorilla.

Understand, oh man! thou art not all soul as are the angels of heaven; nor all flesh and blood as are the brutes, but midway between angels and the brutes—possessing a living *invisible* soul like angels, and *living visible* flesh and blood like brutes. When thou art unkind or selfish, it is the brutish passions within thee which thou hast in common with the brute creation that prompts thee. But when thou doest good things, it is the right knowledge thy soul has *acquired* that prompts thee.

Understand, oh my brother! that every man has *two* lives within him—the *visible* life of the body in *temporary* union with the life of the *invisible* soul. This union of two lives in *one* creature constitutes man. THIS IS THE KEY OF WISDOM.

Every other living creature has but one life, the life of the body.

It is the soul, oh my sister! which gives to man his high capacity for the attainment of knowledge—enabling him, and him alone of all the living creatures in the earth, to comprehend the teachings of God, and to comprehend that the starry skies and all the wondrous things in this round earth were made by a *living* Being, infinitely more powerful and wiser than man.

It is the soul oh my brother! which enables man to comprehend things his eyes cannot see, to comprehend that there are countries of the earth in which he has never set foot, peopled with inhabitants whom he has never seen. It is the soul, oh my sister! which enables thee to comprehend that those wondrous orbs, the comets, come from distant space, so distant that the eye of man cannot see it; that there are, as it were, distant countries in the skies which the eye of man has not beheld; and to comprehend that the Creator of the wondrous orbs that spangle the starry skies is a living Being, invisible to the eyes of man, but not more invisible than thine own self-will nor the air surrounding you; a living Being full of love, full of wisdom, and full of might. Full of love for thee, oh my brother! and for thee, oh my sister! He has shown some of his love in creating thee, man; again showing it in having given thee intellectual power to comprehend His teachings, that He might carry thy worshipping soul into heaven, and be as the angels of heaven for ever, where there is neither pain nor sorrow, but perpetual peace and happiness.

Understand, oh my brother! thy flesh and blood is not like God, thy body has not the shape of God, nor has it the shape of the angels of heaven, but thy living soul is after the likeness of God, in that it is invisible. Understand, oh my sister! the shape of thy soul is not the shape of thy body, for a living man who has lost a leg, or an arm, or an eye, or flesh or blood, or hair or nails, loses naught of his soul, therefore as thou canst not tell the shape of his unseen soul, neither canst thou imagine the shape of God. Bow not down, therefore, oh my brother, nor you, oh my sister, before aught that man foolishly represents as after the image of God, for God deems himself dishonoured thereby; be not thou foolish and tied to the things made by man, like unto the foolish uses of imaginary images and imaginary pictures.

Understand, oh my brother! thy soul is immortal, living for ever after the death of thy body. Understand, oh my sister! that the life of the body is the mere mechanical motion of the heart, which is transmitted from one generation to another; while the heart beats that is life, when its motion is stopped that is death. The flesh, the blood, the bones, the nerves, and all things appertaining to the body of living creatures, and of man, are of earth; and understand, oh my brother! that so long as the earth exists will remain within the earth,—like as a once living tree when burnt is no longer even part of a tree, but changed entirely, its constituents becoming mixed with, and forming part of other things. But the invisible soul, which is in *temporary* union with the living body of man, being part of that living breath of God which He united to the body of Adam, is not of the earth but of heaven. It is a *living substance*, part of the ever-living breath of God, therefore it is immortal, and by its immortality differing from all else within the earth.

Understand, oh my brother! that the living soul, which gives intelligence to the living body of man, separates from the body instantly the motion of the heart stops, and the still ever-living soul is carried by an unseen power out of this orb, never to return; and understand, oh my sister! that when you see the corpse of a man you do not see a man, but the earthly house which once contained a *still* living soul. After thy death, oh my Christian brother! and you, oh my Christian sister! thy still living soul will have no debasing flesh and blood clinging to it, and although incapable of being seen by man, yet is seen of God and His glorious Son, and by the holy angels in heaven; full of intelligence, for God will then add largely to thy worshipping soul in heaven; quick to understand, holy in all things, like unto them.

Understand, oh my brother! in like manner as the living body requires food to sustain it, so the ever-living soul requires food to invigorate it—without mental food the soul would starve, and be void of understanding as a horse or mule. God has made vegetation to grow, and the briny waters of the seas to become pure for the sustenance of living vegetation, and for the sustenance of the flesh and blood of living creatures; and understand, oh my sister! God has also provided *pure* food for the sustenance of the living soul of man, which food are the utterances of God. Men feed the soul when they talk, when they listen, when they read, and when they write; they feed the soul when reading books, not by eating with their teeth the books, but by impressing their contents upon the brain, that photographic plate and storehouse of the soul, so that the living soul grows in knowledge in like manner as the living body grows in stature, each having a different species of food—the food eaten by the teeth giving no sustenance to the soul, because the soul being spiritual, invisible, intangible, feeds only upon what is invisible to the eyes of man and intangible to his touch.

Remember that while man lives upon the earth, the brain, that storehouse of the soul, is filled with *acquired* knowledge, good and bad—that only is good which is a right knowledge of God, and that only is right knowledge which is in accordance with the Holy Bible, for that Book only of all the books which men have read bears the impress of God, bearing it as clearly as the starry skies exhibit the handiwork of God.

Neither the instinct of animals, nor the knowledge of earthly things which men acquire, is true wisdom—true wisdom is a right knowledge of God, which leads to true religion.

CHAPTER II.

God.

MEN mark the small intelligence of the fowls of the air, the creatures of the earth, and the fishes of the waters, so that we are able quickly to distinguish the things which they have made from those that are the handiwork of man, and we behold around us on every side wondrous things—the hills and valleys, the waters, vegetation, living creatures in endless variety, the sun, the moon, and stars. These wondrous things men know came not by chance, but like their ships and houses were created for a purpose, and being created must have been made by a *living* Being, infinitely wiser and infinitely mightier than man—this *living* wondrous Being men call God.

Man also sees that everywhere throughout the earth all things are created most perfectly, and have been maintained in perfect order ever since man's earliest records, therefore men are convinced that God is all-seeing, all-powerful, perfect in wisdom, and everywhere at the same instant of time, governing all things.

CHAPTER III.

What is True Religion?

RELIGION is belief in an unseen God, the creator of all things, who is everywhere, throughout all space, all-powerful, all wise; and belief in the immortality of the soul of man, worshiping God thus believing.

Worship is speaking reverently to the unseen God, believing Him to be close at hand listening.

CHAPTER IV.

EVIDENCES OF THE EXISTENCE OF GOD.

WHEN we see a ship, or railway engine, or clock, or waggon, or balloon sailing in the air, we know they did not come into existence haphazard, but were designed and laboriously made by the hands of man. You would pity the stupidity of the man who tried to convince you that they came suddenly into this round world, no one knowing how or whence they came. The man would be equally stupid who tried to convince us that the wondrous sun, the moon, this round earth with its marvellous contents, and the starry skies, came into existence haphazard,—for they bear the strongest evidence of design and of unity, for some special purpose, as strong as any of the works of man.

Understand, my friend, the stupendous size of the glittering orbs which spangle the starry skies. Our round earth, the orb on which we live, is about 24,000 miles round; the moon is also large and distant from the earth about 240,000 miles; the sun is distant about 93,000,000 of miles from the earth, and of a bulk about 1,477,000 times greater than the round earth. The round stars also, which spangle the skies in millions, are also immensely large, and every one many millions of miles away from the star nearest to it, each appearing small because of the immense distance from us.

Now consider, oh man! the mechanism of a clock, which is the highest effort of the ingenuity of man; it is strictly made according to that law of God known as mechanics. The several parts are not adjusted one to the other haphazard, like unto a heap of loose sand, but strictly according to that law; yet so imperfect is man's knowledge of any of the laws of God that the time-piece of man is but a feeble imitation of God's stupendous time-piece, which is the starry skies. The time-piece of man moves but for a short time, then stops; but the time-piece of God has moved unerringly for about 6000 years. The sun is as the clock-face, the swaying of the moon northward and southward of the earth, swaying to and fro once every lunar month, as the pendulum. The daily revolution of the round earth upon its own axis as the minute-hand, and the one revolution of the earth round the sun during each year, as the hour-hand; and behold the planets and stars and comets, also mark the flight of time, the one as it were testing the accuracy of every other orb, and registering long intervals of time—nothing haphazard, but all having peculiar orbits to produce peculiar effects.

Our common sense tells us that some *living* Being, as superior to man as the infinite largeness of the starry skies is greater than the house of a man, must have wisely designed and made them, constantly watching over them and keeping them in their proper places, and maintaining the exactitude of their motions; for do we not behold spring and summer, autumn and winter following each other with great regularity year after year? And do we not see the moon and this round earth daily moving with great and uniform velocity, mid-day and mid-night occurring every twenty-four hours? The celestial bodies although moving so rapidly making no noise, nothing ever going wrong, no one star or comet ever out of its proper place, no star ever interfering with any other of the millions of stars; everywhere perpetual change, perfect harmony, and perfect peace! Divine mechanism infinitely superior to the time-piece of man. Constant proofs of a mighty unseen *living* Being holding them in check and guiding their movements.

Observe, oh man! concerning the living creatures of the earth, how plainly they also bear the stamp of being the handiwork of the *living* God! how plainly they reveal his wisdom and creative power! Note well the fact, that God has designed and given to every lesser living creature that wondrous inherent knowledge—instinct—exactly suited to its position; each species having its own peculiar food, and instinctively knowing what is hurtful. The young sucking or feeding intuitively, as intuitively as it walks, or flies, or swims; every species after a fashion of its own. Those intended for the water taking to the water, those intended for the air flying in the air, those intended for the land keeping on the land. Every species keeping itself apart from every other species, so that every species is as pure as when God made the first pair of each, although climate has varied them, like as every species of vegetation, and as men vary in appearance, size, and colour. Every member about a creature is marvellously best adapted for what is required of it, therein exhibiting plain evidence of design and the great wisdom of God. The size and position of the teeth, the ears, the mouth, the nose, the tongue, the eyes, the head, the body, the legs, the feet, and the tail, in all their varieties exquisitely adapted for every living creature—for those that walk, or run, or climb, or fly, or swim, or wade; each finding food most suitable for it, the food of one often poisonous to the other, yet each instinctively keeps to its proper food, like its parents. The birds of the air migrating during the darkness of the night, erring not, knowing instinctively their course, every successive generation, neither gaining an increase of instinct nor losing it, but everything as at the creation.

And behold, oh man! how marvellously God has separated every species from every other species—not in outward shape only, but inwardly, and in colour. Note the beauteous markings of the hairy skin, the rich plumage and delicate feathers of the birds, the scaly covering of the finny tribes, and the delicate hues and markings of the leaves and flowers. The songs of the singing birds, and the other utterances of the living creatures—all inwardly and outwardly, in shape and colour, each like their ancestors. As men see and hear them now, so saw and heard our forefathers.

Marvellous, indeed are the living things of the earth, marvellous in their instinct, marvellous in their structure, marvellous in their growth, marvellous in their beauty, marvellous in the adaptation of their several parts, and marvellous in the perpetuation of colour, but not more marvellous than the perfect separation of the species one from the other, from generation to generation.

And mark, oh man! the evidences of one great plan in the multiplication of living things, and how the males equal in number the females, the manner of their birth varying ;—God delighting to exhibit marvellous variety in all things. Living creatures, having both father and mother; living vegetation, having vegetation for their father and earth for their mother; and the living things which link living creatures with living vegetation, multiplying by separation of their own living selves, having no mother, in like manner as the first infant Eve, was born out of the first man Adam, and had no mother. And note, oh man! that when man and all living creatures, and all living vegetation were created, God placed within the males, as part of themselves, seed within seed, in circles innumerable, that all the seed might not be born into the world at one time, but at intervals, throughout many generations. The sleeping life in the seed of vegetation, finding food suitable to its development and activity in the ground, its nursing mother; and sleeping life in the seed of each species of living creature, finding food suitable for its development and activity only in the female of its own species, thus maintaining every species of living creature distinct from every other species.

And mark, oh man! the wondrous unseen machinery of a living creature! The skin and opacity of the flesh hide the many moving parts from thy curious eyes. Thou canst not see the pumping heart, the flowing of the blood through numberless tubes, the play of the muscles, the action of the nerves, photographing thoughts, and smells, and feelings, and sights, upon the delicate nerves in the brain. Thou canst not see the transformings that are going on within the living creature, vegetation and flesh being converted into bone, into hair, into muscle, into nerves, into blood, and the many diverse liquids and parts within them—all these take place within thee, oh man! and in every living creature; but thou canst not see them; they are invisible to all earthly eyes, as God Himself. How clumsy are the machines of man, compared to that wondrous machine, a living creature. Like as the steam machines of man derive motion from fire and water, so the living body maintains its inward motion from the food it swallows. The machines of man require the supervision of the soul of man to control and direct them; but God has given to living machines, His creatures, inherent hereditary power to control and direct their own movements and promptings, to take food, and to perpetuate their kind.

And behold, oh man! the unity of design, as seen in the marvellous links between things that are animate from those that have no life. Mark well the great gulf for *ever* fixed between man and the gorilla—that brute whose shape is most like the shape of man—and note the gradation from the gorilla downward; and the gradation from the living creatures which walk the earth to living creatures that fly, and with living creatures which inhabit the waters; also the gradation between living creatures that walk the earth, and that swim, with those that creep; and the gradation between living creatures that creep, with those that bore; and between those that are free to roam, and those that are fixtures—doubtful to the mind, some of them, whether they be living creatures or living plants. Then note, oh man! the gradation between living plants and things which never had life within them, which neither grow nor die, link within link innumerable, imperceptibly, from the gorilla to a stone. The one never changing permanently into another, but every species maintained distinct, generation after generation. As were the first species at the Creation, so are they now—unchangeable for ever—the lion never becoming a horse, nor the horse a lion.

And behold, oh man! how marvellously God has designed that wondrous machine the body of living creatures. Like as the steam machines of man derive motion from fire and water, so the living body maintains its motion from the food it swallows. The machines of man require the supervision of the soul of man to control and direct them, but God has given to the living body inherent hereditary power to control and direct its own movements, giving it instinct and sense. And mark, oh man! how wondrously God has given to the body of all living creatures promptings to eat, to drink, to sleep, and the many other promptings, not haphazard and without an object, but absolutely necessary, every prompting exactly adapted to the purpose which God designed, promptings not left to self-will, but forced at times against ignorant self-will, overruling it. In like manner as the time-piece of God excels the time-piece of man, so the mechanism of the body of every living creature excels the highest efforts of man's machinery. Herein is the infinite wisdom of God made plain to human understanding.

And behold the marvellous waters of the briny deep—how came they salt? Why do they ever remain neither more salt nor less, no more in quantity nor less? Why do they so largely cover the surface of the earth? In like manner as vegetation is necessary for the sustenance of man, so are the briny waters necessary for the sustenance of every living thing. From the very first God made the sea salt, as salt as now, that the dead habiters of the waters might not pollute the air nor pollute the water; it was necessary the sea should be salt, that the dead things therein might not corrupt. God peopled the briny deep with living creatures, in like manner as He has peopled the land. And behold how extensively the briny seas cover the surface of the earth, that the sun might cause pure watery vapour, in large quantities, to ascend out of the seas, to give variety above, and shower down pure water upon the thirsty soil throughout the earth, and provide running streams for the sustenance of every living thing. The salt adapted to the water, and the briny seas adapted to the extent of the habitable land—marvellous evidence of one grand unity of design!

And behold how many things are necessary to the existence of every living thing. First, the existence of the *living* God, the wise Creator; then are necessary the sun, and moon, and earth; then the motions of the earth, and the motion of the moon; then that the earth should be habitable; then of the air we breathe; then of the briny seas of great extent to produce clouds, that streams and springs of pure water throughout the habitable land might give sustenance to every living thing, and that the soil might be pulverized and moistened frequently, neither to be too long dry nor too long wet; the hills and the valleys, that there might be streams and springs; then the heat and cold, day and night; and next the seasons. Then that vegetation should have power to grow and multiply, that part might be food, and part as ornaments to the habitable land, to give it beauty; then that living creatures should be able to see, or feel, or hear, or move, and have growth, and have power to multiply their species; those intended for the briny seas adapted to the seas; those intended for the streams adapted to the streams; those intended to walk, or creep, or bore, adapted to the earth; and those intended for the air furnished with wings; all necessities of existence, as necessary as birth into the world; as necessary as that living things should feed for a time then disappear from the face of the earth, that the earth might not be crowded; but not more necessary than that God should love us, and pity our follies, and seek to enlighten us by giving us His Holy Scriptures, and touch our hearts while tracing out the evidence of His wisdom and His love.

Everything upon this earth is as harmoniously made as are the sun, moon, and stars.
sun, moon, and stars.

Consider these things, oh man ! and commune with thine heart respecting these wondrous acts of God !

And behold ! the moon designedly placed exactly at the proper distance from the earth and maintained there, producing with the sun,—winds, rain-clouds, and ocean-tides, that vegetation might receive moisture, and that neither air nor the waters might corrupt, nor become stagnant; neither too far away nor too near, that the winds may neither be too little nor too great, nor the rains, nor the tides.

And behold ! the earth designedly placed exactly at the most suitable distance from the sun, and maintained there throughout all ages, that the extremes of heat and cold might not be too great for the life of living creatures. The moon and earth and sun, varying in their distances the one from the other just so much as to produce a pleasant variety between year and year— God not permitting the moon to come nearer to the round earth that it may not again be deluged with water, so that the living creatures upon the face of the earth may not again be destroyed, nor permitting the round earth to go so near the vast burning sun as to be utterly consumed by fire, nor too far away as that all things that have life should not lose life by cold. Man has no fear, believing that He who designed and made them also governs them, therefore confidently makes his arrangements for the morrow.

And behold ! the motions of the round earth and the motions of the moon around the earth are in exact obedience to certain *fixed* laws. Now understand, oh man ! and keep it always in thy remembrance—where there are laws there must be design. Every living creature exists in accordance with certain *fixed* laws—laws that are unchangeable ; all things that are inanimate are made according to certain other fixed laws.

These laws are those of chemistry, the law of mechanics, the law of life and death, and the like. Well, who made those laws—all plain evidences of unity of design, not one clashing with another, but all graduating most harmoniously one into another? Man has not *made* one; he has simply very imperfectly *discovered* a few which God has laid down—discovering them as he discovers grains of gold beneath the surface of the earth. Well, who made those laws which exhibit wisdom infinitely superior to the wisdom of man?

The author of those laws is God Himself, the great unseen Being, our loving Father, our wise Creator.

And consider, oh man! this round earth in which we live is about 24,000 miles round—a round ball turning *once* upon its axis during twenty-four hours, never varying, never backward nor forward, but completes one turn exactly every twenty-four hours, thereby producing one day and one night, the outer part exposed to the light of the sun being the day thereof, and the outer part that is not shone upon by the sun being the night thereof. Men stand upon the round earth with their feet pulled towards its centre, like pins stuck towards the centre of a ball. Every man, the waters of the ocean, everything on the surface of the round earth, therefore, travels through a space of about 1000 miles every hour; nevertheless, God has so contrived that this rapid motion should make no noise, and to the things of the round earth be as though it were motionless.

A wondrous act of God! but not more wondrous than any of His other works—every living creature, every living plant as marvellous—exhibiting design, power, and wisdom beyond the comprehension of man!

Friend! hast thou studied with the microscope the wondrous wisdom of God as revealed in the marvellously small and innumerable living creatures that exist unseen to the unassisted eye —in like manner as the air we breathe and as God Himself is unseen—which are as active, full of life, feel pleasure and pain, and as fearful of danger as thyself? Invisible to the naked eye, requiring a microscope to see them, the greater the power of the microscope the greater the number of minute living creatures are revealed, revealing to the wondering eyes the creative power of God extended to *living* creatures illimitable in their minuteness.

And behold, oh man! the cloudless starry firmament, the handiwork of God. View with thine eyes the countless stars; are they not glorious? Behold the thin white clouds that are here and there interspersed far, far away amid the stars. Take to thyself a telescope, and note well, that what appeared to thine unassisted eyes as thin white clouds, the telescope reveals as clusters of stars innumerable, immensely distant; and lo! with thy telescope thou canst see other thin white clouds unseen before by thine unassisted eyes. Take yet a second telescope, the most powerful man has made, and behold! these second white clouds are also clusters of stars innumerable; and lo! elsewhere come to view other third white clouds so immensely distant as to be unseen by the first telescope, these also are clusters of stars innumerable, but there is no telescope able to distinguish them; yet each of these starry balls which reflect the brilliant electric light of the sun are several thousands of miles in diameter, and there is a vacuous space of many millions of miles between each star and its nearest neighbour. The telescopes of man reveal millions of stars that are invisible to the unassisted eye, so distant as to be like bright pin-points, so numerous and apparently close together as the particles of sand upon a sandy shore.

The more man searches into space the greater marvels he beholds, enticing him to search more deeply still. His most powerful microscopes leave still unrevealed the actual size of the most minute *living* creature God has made; his most powerful telescope equally leaves unrevealed the actual extent of the starry firmament. The wisest man is confounded at both extremes. It is equally beyond the power of man to comprehend the vastness of the starry firmament as to comprehend the minuteness of an atom, or to comprehend the internal collective weight of the countless stars, or to comprehend the weight of an atom of that electric heat which is constantly poured into our round world from the vast burning sun.

The wise man is filled with awe by these revelations of the infinite wisdom, power and goodness of God. He feels his littleness in the presence of One so mighty in all things; but the fool, thoughtless, void of understanding—apparently as a four-footed beast, unaware of *his* littleness—is conceited, refuses to bow the knee and worship the wondrous unseen God, but is afraid of spirits, that have no existence, that never did exist, being like heathen mythology, the stupid inventions of cunning men. Or a working man, for a livelihood, makes an image of a man upon a cross—an image, having a head, body, legs, arms, fingers, and toes, the same as has the brute gorilla; a priest of the Papacy—a false, impious sect, followers of adulterated Scripture—makes a stupid sign over it; a fool is taught from his infancy to regard it (in consequence of the false priest making the stupid sign) as a sacred image, and as a likeness of God; and is taught to use it as a *necessary* part of his worship, to carry it about his person; he bows down before it, uttering prayers; venerates it as a holy thing, kisses it, fondly clasping it as his eyes close in death;—deceived through life by the priest and his own thoughtlessness, as though God and His Glorious Son had never been revealed;—a lost soul for ever!

CHAPTER V.

Why we cannot see God.

GOD in His wisdom has made the eyes of all living earthly creatures so that we can neither see the air we breathe, nor see Him, nor that invisible *living* cloud, the Holy Spirit of God, which, proceeding from God, and being part of Himself (in like manner as the wings of a bird proceed from its body)* is everywhere throughout space.

If He were visible, the great and vivid light of His Holy Person would perpetually obscure the infinitely lesser light of the vast burning sun, nor would the moon nor countless stars be seen, nor change of seasons. God's great light and Holy Spirit would obscure all other things, and blind our eyes. The living creatures in this world are differently constituted to the holy angels in heaven; what to them is life, would to us be death. It was, therefore, a necessity that the eyes of living creatures should be unable to see God. In the place of His intense light He has given man and all earthly things the infinitely lesser light of the burning sun, the candle of the starry skies; for no unholy living creature is permitted to see the light that comes from the Person of God Himself. God has provided earthly things with a temporary substitute for Himself in the vast burning sun which He made for the purpose.

God made the sun to be a large, dense, cold ball, which slowly burns on the outside (like as a candle burns), and gives light and warmth. He has made it of that hardest and densest of all substances, *latent heat*, which is heat in a state of rest, therefore having no warmth.

This substance is constantly maintained by the power of God in a state of unrest on the surface of the sun, being there converted from a cold solid into a thin fiery gas, which, being strongly attracted by the earth, moon, and stars, flies to them; a portion enters the outside of the round earth, and there combines, more or less, with everything, in accordance with a law of God, giving warmth; then becoming rested, solidifies, becoming cold as when forming part of the sun. The surface of the earth, therefore, always contains more latent heat than the interior of the earth : the nearer to the centre of the earth, the greater is the difference. This difference in the quantity of latent heat causes a strong attractive force between that which has much and that which has less :—this pulling force towards the fixed centre of the earth men call weight.

What God is to the heavenly soul of man, the inanimate sun is to his body, and to all things of the earth. Without the sun, neither man, nor any living creature, nor vegetation, nor hills, nor valleys, nor the earth, nor the moon, nor the stars could exist. It liquifies and solidifies all the things we see. Without it they would be gas, as before the creation. It maintains vitality in all living creatures, and in vegetation; produces their food, lights and warms them with its direct rays, and warms them with its active heat that emanates from the latent heat, in coal, in wood, in oil and fat; produces vivification and change in all things; produces the wood, the stone, and solid metals, and is the only source of weight. What the main spring is to a clock, the sun is to all things that our eyes can see. It is the mainspring of the starry firmament. As man fashions the mainspring of a watch, so God fashioned that great inanimate mainspring, the sun; making the sun, the moon, the stars, the earth, and all things therein, subsidiary to the soul of man; for God made them all for the sake of man, to provide him with a glorious habitation—glorious within and glorious without.

The eyes of man, although far reaching, are imperfect—they cannot see through a brick or solid stone wall, or through any

c

opaque substance ; neither can they see the air we breathe and in which we live, nor see self-will ; nevertheless, common sense tells us we have self-will, and that we move in the midst of air ; because when the air is in motion we see the driven clouds, our garments are blown about us, dust, leaves, and other substances are whirled before it, and the wide waters are lashed into great waves. We thus see the effects produced by air in motion, although we cannot see the air itself; so in like manner we can see the evidences of God's handiwork, although we cannot see God Himself.

We cannot see God, but everywhere we see the works of His hands—the sun, the moon, the countless stars, and all the wondrous contents of our round world ; in like manner as in our houses we see the works that men have made, yet those men are not visible to us ; nevertheless we feel assured, by our knowledge of the world, that our chairs and tables were made by man, and not by four-footed beasts. So in like manner we can distinguish the works which God has made from those which are the handiwork of man.

Moreover God is the perfection of holiness, is perfectly righteous, is goodness itself; hating with intense hatred every kind of idolatry and wickedness, therefore hating the iniquity of man, keeping His holy Person far away from them that it may be undefiled, yet taking great interest in man, and yearning like as a tender loving mother yearns for her absent child, because distributed among mankind is the soul of Adam, which originally having come from Himself, and having been redeemed by His glorious Son, is holy in His sight, and which He yearns to collect together, and carry into heaven.

Friend, thou hast perhaps seen those great travelling burning suns, the comets, that have visited the starry firmament of late years. They came you know not whence, approached our round earth at a velocity of many millions of miles each day ;

their speed gradually became lessened, and eventually turned away before reaching us; and then gradually accelerating their speed, vanished from our unassisted eyes, and afterwards from our most powerful telescopes, while travelling at several millions of miles each hour, you know not where; finally becoming too minute to be seen, owing to their immense distance—a great invisible living Being silently guiding their way amid the countless stars, without disturbing them, without noise, silent; again to re-appear after an interval of many years, giving proofs to the thoughtful of an immeasurable space our eyes cannot reach.

It is in the midst of this immeasurable space which surrounds the starry skies, that the dwelling of God is fixed—the heaven of infinite space, its centre. He is there in full glory, God in a condensed state as a living Being, seen by His glorious Son and His happy angels; but his holy Spirit, a part of Himself (like as the wings of a bird are part of the bird), an invisible *living* cloud, fills all else of space; so that He is everywhere, and His glorious Son, the happy angels, and all things, live and move and exist in this invisible living cloud surrounding them (as the waters of the sea surround the fishes in the sea), and guiding the motions of the vast burning sun, the moon, the countless stars, the comets, and this round earth; and seeing the movements, and hearing the words, and knowing the secret thoughts of all men; for this invisible living cloud is as it were all eyes and all ears. God is the living sun of heaven. What the inanimate sun is to the starry skies, and to this round earth, God is to the heavens which surround the starry skies; saturating with His living light and love and joy, His glorious Son and all the holy angels of heaven.

We cannot see the Holy Person of God in the heaven of the starry firmament where he dwells, because He is too far off for our eyes to reach Him; in like manner as we cannot see the distant comets. Moreover it is His holy desire we should not see

Him, nor can we see His Holy Spirit, the living invisible cloud that is everywhere, and in which we live and move. Nevertheless our common sense tells us He is everywhere, because we see the moon, the stars, and this round earth moving so harmoniously, nothing ever going wrong; spring, summer, autumn, and winter following each other with great regularity, and the inanimate sun giving growth and change to all the wondrous things on the surface of the earth.

Common sense, therefore, proclaims there is a mighty living Being whom men call God.

CHAPTER VI.

Proofs that God has Communicated with Man.

COMMON sense would naturally expect that this mighty living God having endowed man with greater intelligence than any other living creature (for which of them besides man is capable of deep thought, of speech, of writing, of reading, of acquiring information, and of giving it), should have created the first man, Adam, the human father of all mankind, for some special purpose, and should have made Himself known to Adam, the most intelligent of all things that He had made, in order to explain to him the special purpose for which he was created. This God did to Adam when he made Him.

In Adam were the living germs of every male and female descendant of Adam: all who have lived and may hereafter live. Consider, oh man! a seed of wheat; from one seed thou canst, oh man! as thou knowest, produce millions of other like seed. How minute must be the living germ in each seed, and how marvellously minute must have been the living germ in the wheat which God first created, and which has now continued to live for about 6000 years—for the living principle is in the seed and not in the ground, which simply gives it food wherewith to be sustained: therefore, as is the seed so is the plant, and so is the living creature.

God enshrined in the *living* body of Adam a pure *living* soul—an invisible *living* cloud, which, being invisible, yet alive, was therefore like God—by breathing it into the nostrils of the *living* flesh and blood of Adam, which God had just before made, and the twain—

1. The invisible living soul
2. The visible flesh and blood

were called the man Adam. To Adam only God gave these two lives; to all other living creatures He gave but one life— the life of the flesh and blood. *This is the key of wisdom.* Behold, oh man! in the brute gorilla an image of thyself, as thyself would be if thou hadst not a soul—that jewel from heaven, in which only thou art like God.

God created every kind of living creature before He created Adam—he, the earthly lord of all the round earth, was created the last. Other living creatures were *created*, male and female, a pair of every kind: the male equal to the female, and the female equal to the male: man alone, for God's wise purposes, and in accordance with His grand simple plan, He made male, that, as part of His great plan, there might be but *one* earthly lord of the whole earth. Adam was the last of all things which God created. But God designed that the *one* earthly lord, Adam, should, like all other creatures, have a helpmate worthy of him; and, causing Adam to fall into a deep sleep, He caused the beauteous female infant, Eve, to issue from a rib of Adam. Thus was Eve the first of all *born* creatures, and thus did Eve have no mother: in like manner, as in long years afterwards, the holy Christ had no father.

Out of Adam was *born* the infant Eve, that Adam might be the *one* earthly lord, and the *one* earthly father of all mankind.

Some time afterwards Eve became Adam's wife, and the mother of all mankind. The man Adam, and the female Eve were perfectly happy, and in constant communion with God, keeping the desires of their bodies wholly subject to their holy souls. They were as brother and sister, perfectly happy, as are the angels in heaven; for they then had God always with them, communing with them and teaching them. They were therefore wiser than all their descendants in all things which conduced to their happiness. And all the other living creatures were perfectly happy—the lion and the lamb resting together, eating herbage. There was no fear in all the world. The Lord God having taught them all that was requisite for them to know, was desirous of testing these the chief of all living earthly things; and warning them to keep their bodies, their earthly part, in entire subjection to their souls, their heavenly part, declaring that disobedience to His commands would entail misery upon them—God left them purposely for awhile.

The withdrawal of God induced the rebellion of their flesh and blood, for the temptations of the body overcame the conscience of the soul, and they fell from being holy earthly angels into being angels of sin; for after God had withdrawn Himself, the woman Eve saw the serpent doing that which the Lord God commanded them not to do, the serpent not having been forbidden, because it was a beast of the field. Eve also did it; and tempting Adam, he also did it—and thus both disobeyed God—the first of all living creatures that dared to disobey Him.

Thus was that terrible thing, disobedience to the commands of God, brought into the world; and thus was the happiness of the world wrecked. God foreknew that the *one* earthly lord, Adam, would disobey Him; and God, therefore, in His great fore-ordained plan had provided an everlasting antidote, in the person of His Son Jesus Christ, for the salvation of the living soul of Adam; of that one soul, part whereof has been in every one of his descendants, and part whereof still lives in every human being now alive, having now attained an age of about 6000 years. Therefore, oh my brother! and you, oh my sister! lift up thy voices prayerfully and thankfully to God, for thy earthly misery is but for a little while, and then thou wilt be joyous with God in heaven for ever.

God condemned the flesh and blood of Adam, and the flesh and blood of his descendant Eve, and the flesh and blood of all his other descendants—to live for a time and then ignominiously return, like brute beasts, to the dust whence they were taken. God declared his intention to cease communing with them, for they had polluted their immortal souls and had become angels of sin; but mercifully to mollify their anguish (for keenly they then knew what it was to be good and what to be evil), God foretold that although the dreadful sin of disobedience required the death of the soul of man, as well as the death of his body, yet God had provided an all-sufficient substitute for the salvation of his soul, which substitute should be the offspring of a woman, but not of a man—a riddle which God in His own good time afterwards explained to mean Christ, who in the fulness of time, by His dreadful mediatory death, paid the debt—life for life—giving the holy life of his *body* to save from death the *soul* of Adam, which has been distributed among mankind.

God gave Eve to be the wife of Adam, and upon several occasions afterwards, when mankind had multiplied, the Holy Spirit of God communicated to certain holy men the laws of God, who were sent as His holy messengers to explain His holy laws to mankind generally.

Some of the holy men, honoured as the mouth-pieces of the unseen God, were notably Noah, Abraham, Isaac, Jacob, Moses, David, and Christ. God's messages have been handed down to us in the words of holy men, and these writings have been collected in one book; this book is called the holy Scriptures, being a sacred record of God's dealings, from the creation of the vast burning sun, the moon, the countless stars, and this round earth, down to the death of the Apostles of Jesus Christ; the latest record being about 1800 years ago; since which time there have been no prophets, no divinely-appointed living messengers; God having then revealed to man all that is necessary for him to know for the salvation of his soul from death. The whole record of the Holy Scriptures extend over a period of about 4000 years; they are the only written messages of God to man—they are now the only Divinely appointed messengers of God. Holy men are now but teachers of the Word of God—not messengers, but teachers only; simply imparting their knowledge of the laws of God to others having less knowledge—like unto teachers of earthly things.

Our common sense naturally expects proofs that these holy men were really messengers of God.

The Holy Scriptures teem with proofs. God being perfectly holy, we should naturally suppose that His mouth-pieces would be the very best—not second best—but the very best and holiest of mankind; men long known to their nation as the holiest of men; lovers of truth, God-fearing men, recognized by their countrymen as inspired by God. Well then, the Holy Scriptures are records written by these holiest of men.

Our common sense would naturally expect that the utterances of these holy men would testify in some peculiar way that they were really mouth-pieces of God, not only to men of their time, but also to mankind who should live thereafter; for how otherwise could mankind know they were not impostors, like the blasphemous priests of the Papacy of these times, who impudently pretend to hold the keys of heaven and hell, and falsely pretend to be mediators between God and man, and thereby claim (the cunning worldly men) supreme direction over the affairs of the whole world, and yet can really do nothing beyond what any other men can do.

The utterances of those holy men of old bear the stamp of truth in all they said, their wisdom is far beyond that of all other men. God, through them, has declared to mankind how to distinguish His mouth-pieces from those who, like the priests of the Papacy, are simply weak-minded or cunning impostors.

He has declared that His servants really appointed by Him shall be esteemed the holiest of men, abhor the use of images in their worship of God, be humble, seeking not their own glorification, and by miracles which shall be done in the sight of many men, and by prophecies which shall come to pass, be convincing proofs, to both onlookers and to men in after generations, that they were truly the mouth-pieces of God, and that men who could not show such credentials were not appointed by God.

The Holy Spirit of God performed wondrous miracles in their behalf. He also put into their minds the power to foretell events that should take place; some in a few days, some in a few years, some after the lapse of many hundred years— prophecies which were fulfilled, not one jot nor one tittle remaining unfulfilled of those numerous prophecies of whose fulfilment the time has elapsed. These wondrous acts being witnesses to all men of the truthful sayings of these holy men. Miracles which no man of himself could possibly perform being witnesses of their truth to onlookers, and to men of their generation: prophecies to after generations of men.

Are you doubtful about miracles?

Is not the self-will of every living creature a miracle? Is not their instinct a miracle? Is not everything around us, in the air and in the earth, a miracle? Is not the impossibility of seeing the most minute *living* creature, even with the aid of the most powerful microscope, marvellous? Is not life marvellous, and death also? Are not comets miracles? Is not the diurnal motion of the earth, causing the whole surface of the earth and all things thereon to revolve at the rate of about 24,000 miles every twenty-four hours, without the slightest noise, without the least disturbance of the air surrounding us, a marvel utterly beyond the comprehension of man? Is not the regular motion of the moon, swaying like a pendulum while revolving round the earth, swaying once to and fro every lunar month, a marvel? The earth revolves once every twenty-four hours upon its own axis, producing day and night, meanwhile the axis very slowly oscillates, each pole moving alternately inwards and outwards towards the sun, somewhat like a pendulum, occupying one year to complete one oscillation, thereby producing the pleasant changes of spring, summer, autumn, and winter during each oscillation, also producing the gradual lengthening of the days, and then the gradual shortening of the days : exhibiting thoughtful arrangement, peculiar motions being given to produce peculiar effects, just as a time-piece shows thoughtful arrangement in the mind of the man who made it.

Are not these motions of the earth a miracle? Is not the very presence in the skies of the sun, the earth, and those moving stars the planets, and the countless fixed stars, each surrounded by nothing, weighing nothing, possessing great weight inwardly, but outwardly nothing, flashing the light of the sun, each like an electric spark, a miracle?

Yes, indeed these are marvellous, grand miracles, worthy of God the Most High. What are the lesser marvels of God :—the bringing out of heaven the soul of the Holy Angel Christ, enshrining it in the living flesh and blood of an unborn child that was issuing out of the womb of the Virgin Mary, the restoration of the dead to life, the instantaneous healing of the sick, the foretelling what would come to pass, and the other marvels narrated in Scripture—to those grand miracles?

Recollect, oh man! there were times in the history of the world when God deemed it advisable to make certain things known to man, which man, left to his own resources, could not possibly know. Man could not possibly know ought about God—not being able to see Him, nor hear His voice, nor know His wishes, nor His intentions, nor whether there was only one God or many Gods, whether there was such a place as heaven, or such a place as hell, or that man possessed an *immortal* soul—unless God by some means told him. God therefore selected certain holy men to be His messengers; He put into their minds holy thoughts, and prompted them to give them utterance; also prompted them to prophecy certain things which God knew would come to pass, and also prompted them to command certain things to be done which things God had not given power for men to do, that were deemed impossible to be done, but which God, unseen by men, did as though they were done by the will of the holy messengers. These miracles being performed by God to convince the people that the holy messengers were not impostors, but His appointed servants.

These holy messengers were not jugglers—who mystify by nimbleness of fingers, or by the aid of confederates, or by fraud, or by ingenuity,—but by the mouth they simply gave utterance, and what they said the Holy Spirit of God did.

A simple arrangement, simple and grand, as are all the works of God!

Common sense would also naturally require proofs of great wisdom in their sayings and writings.

The proofs are in the wonderful wisdom and accuracy of those holy records—the Scriptures.

The holy writers lived in times when communication with far-distant nations was unknown : times, when the inhabitants of many vast countries were unheard of; when superstition, absurdities, fabulous legends and error everywhere were rife; when chemistry, geology, the world's history, the sciences generally, were all but unknown; when every nation was, through false priests, steeped in idolatry and lies : nevertheless, these holy men, living at intervals embracing about 2000 years, were filled with true wisdom, and had a knowledge of God far surpassing all other men, and have been models of uprightness through many generations down to these days, were notoriously the most pious and holiest of men, and were unanimous in their sayings, not contradicting each other, but as it were of one mind. They worshipped but one God—at times in the open air, at times in an ordinary house, at times in the sanctuary, abhorred the use of images in their worship: neither did they worship reputed saints, nor angels, nor were they superstitious about them; heeded not whether they wore this peculiar garment or that; sought not their own glorification, nor case, nor worldly comfort, nor the reverence of men—yet men accorded them great reverence—being convinced they were truly the mouth-pieces of God.

Moses describes the creation of the vast burning sun, the moon, the countless stars, and this round world, in a way that no man could of himself, even in these scientific days, have originally explained, without divine assistance—for embodied in his description is the very height of knowledge in every science; and yet Moses lived in an age when ignorance of science was universal, and had been always so.

Moses tells us that all men are descended from *one* man, Adam—the man whom God created at the beginning—God giving to him, and to all other living creatures, perfect freedom of action, not controlling them, but controlling the motion of the inanimate sun, the moon, the countless stars, and this round earth; and that Adam, and the first-born Eve, his wife, disobeyed God, and so afterwards did their descendants, who attained great stature and lived to a great age, and were therefore clever in worldly things, and who became very numerous and wicked, in forgetting God, and unteachable, as though they had no more spiritual understanding than four-footed creatures; so that after the round earth had been made about 1600 years, God resolved to destroy them, along with all living creatures, excepting a few of each kind, and Noah's family, that the world might be peopled afresh, so that God might more successfully influence mankind to do His will.

Moses records that, about 1600 years after the creation of

Adam, the man Noah, the only holy man then alive of all the giant men who then thickly inhabited the earth, was commanded by God to build a large ship, without masts, called an ark, and to enter therein, with his family, taking with him an allotted few of each species of living creature, and there to continue for a certain time the messenger of God, declaring it to be the intention of God to deluge the whole world with water, and thereby destroy all the creatures that inhabited the surface of the round earth, excepting those that were in the ark.

Moses records that a deluge of water came upon the earth with great violence, uprooting and destroying the living creatures, thoroughly destroying all traces of the colossal works of wicked man, and completely altering the surface of the whole earth, the waters having rolled over the highest mountains; and that the deluge lasted many days.

The Lord God in His holy anger caused the moon to go much nearer to the round earth, and remain there during forty days and forty nights, that the solid surface of the earth might be disrupted and swell out and become the liquid water, that the water might deeply cover the whole surface of the ground, covering the highest mountains, to drown all the living creatures excepting those in the ark with Noah.

Understand, oh man! the round earth has a bulk about forty-nine times greater than that of the moon, and therefore is more saturated with solar heat than is the moon. The moon contains less solar heat, in proportion to its bulk, than does the earth. Therefore understand, oh man! that when the Lord God placed the moon much nearer to the round earth; the ground and waters of the earth, the dormant solar heat within the round earth and the moon, became together, as it were, a great and powerful galvanic battery; for the dormant solar heat which solidified the ground, quickly loosened and sped towards the moon, the round earth becoming, as it were, a sun to the moon, and the whole surface of the ground became quickly split and disrupted, and great chasms were made in the shallow oceans. Great clouds of vapour arose from the fast decomposing ground and the fast decomposing mountains, during the time the moon was nearer to the round earth, which turned into rain in quantity sufficient to cover to a great depth with water the whole surface of the round earth—the waves rolling over the highest mountains. The solid surface of the round earth and the solid surface of the mountains were converted into water, and the mountains dwindled greatly.

The Lord God, after forty days and forty nights, removed back the moon, which caused the round earth to be no longer, as it were, a sun to the moon, and decomposition of the ground and of the mountains ceased; and gradually the oxygen and hydrogen of the superfluous waters entered into fresh combinations with the only other earthly element, nitrogen; the solar heat again became dormant, and they solidified once more into earthy and metallic matter, which settled, with the sweepings of the oceans and of the old continents and islands to the bottom of the water, into strata. The waters were many days shrinking into the comparatively small quantity that now forms the waters of the round earth.

The superfluous waters shrank from off the face of the higher ground, and left dry new continents and new islands, much like as we now see them. Noah, his family, and all the living creatures in the ark, then left it, and thenceforth lived according as they willed.

CHAPTER VII.

PROOFS THAT THE BIBLICAL RECORD OF THE DELUGE IS TRUE.

OF the truth of this wonderful narrative by Moses we have innumerable proofs. The vast sandy deserts, and the peculiar formation of every hill, every plain, and the appearance of every mountain, throughout the world, all bear the strongest proofs, and proofs innumerable, of *one* mighty universal deluge.

The highest mountains throughout the world are silent witnesses, in the large quantities of sea shells and of alluvial matter deposited upon them, now formed into concrete stony masses, of their having been deposited by violently agitated water which reached their topmost pinnacles. Every hill and every valley are formed out of the sweepings of the ancient seas, and of ancient continents and islands, in strata of great thickness, separately, of shells, of gravel, of sand, of trees, of mud, and other matter, some since converted into concrete stony masses and coal—the lowermost resting on the Adamite and granite rocks, whose surface, for the most part, is greatly below the water-level of existing seas, the highest strata towering, for the most part, far above the present ocean-tides.

When the Lord God had put back the moon, and thereby stopped the further disruption of the surface of the round earth, then, during calms, the earthy matter suspended in the water began to fall, forming thick strata—the heaviest first and the mud last—storms sweeping them out of the seas in masses upon what God intended should be dry land, until the seas were clean swept and nothing lost in them.

During the deluge tropical trees, and the remains of tropical creatures, were removed by the waters thousands of miles, and afterwards sank upon far distant lands.

Man since the deluge knew nothing about that huge beast

the mastodon, until about 150 years ago, when the remains of one were found deeply buried in the ground—buried during the deluge. Numbers of these gigantic, once living, hairless, tropical beasts have since been found frozen up in sand banks, retaining all their flesh and original form almost unchanged, in the frozen regions. One was also found in the icy regions, embedded in a mass of ice, whose flesh was still sweet when found, and eaten when given to dogs, having been preserved by the frozen waters ever since the deluge, now about 4000 years.

Are not these things silent witnesses of the great deluge, and of the truth of Moses? Is not their preservation miraculous?

The present appearance of the hill containing the tomb of Abraham—who was born about 290 years after the deluge, while Noah was yet alive—and Jacob's well; of hills and valleys, and rivers, and of the Red sea—all of which so exactly correspond in these days with the description thereof by Moses, that common sense must of necessity come to the conclusion that the general aspect of the surface of the whole earth has altered but very little since the great deluge, subsidence and upheaval having taken place in only a very few comparatively small spots in the world. About 4000 years have elapsed since the days of Abraham. Moreover, buildings now exist that were erected near to the time of Abraham, and these very buildings are described by the most ancient historians as the most ancient of their time; these handiworks of man have therefore proved very durable. The absence of more ancient ones in the days of the most ancient historians, proves the truth of the records of Moses, that the deluge destroyed all the works of men's hands—destroyed all signs of their existence.

The wonderfully concise and clear way the narrative is told is another strong proof of its truth. No man has since, even in these scientific days, been able to give a different account, that will bear investigation, for the existence of hills and valleys, and undulating strata of the earth, built up with transported materials; for the presence of masses of sea-shells on the tops of the highest mountains, or for the thick deposit of *tropical* trees, transported thousands of miles, which have since been converted into coal, having thick strata of earthy matter, sometimes containing the remains of tropical animals interspersed between the layers of coal; for the presence of immensely thick strata of clay, sand, shells, concrete mud, and gravel, which are found everywhere on the surface of the whole earth —miraculously, I say, miraculously piled one above the other —forming high land, sometimes a series of high hills, like huge waves far above the ocean tides, none having apparently been wasted in the depths of the ocean, but the ocean clean swept to form high land and to cover the Adamite and granitic inner part of the round earth; or for the presence of the long-extinct tropical mastodons in the icy regions.

The absurd attempts of rash scientific men to give a different explanation are proofs that Moses derived his knowledge from God alone. How otherwise could he, living in times of universal ignorance, have given a description which we find so accurate, and have acquired earthly knowledge so vastly superior to other men.

CHAPTER VIII.
Other Proofs of Bible Truth.

ANOTHER proof of the accuracy of the Holy Scriptures is shown by the earthy formation situated between the uneven granitic rocks—uneven as a mountain range—forming the inner structure of the round earth, and the vast heaps of transported earthy and vegetable matter which were deposited by the Deluge upon those rocks.

The strong vitality which mankind possessed before the Deluge, when men attained the great age of nearly 1000 years, extended to all other living creatures and to vegetation; these, like Adam, attained great age and colossal stature, owing to the strong vitality of their new-made life, and thickly covered at the time of the Deluge the whole earth; for, owing to the paucity of deaths and slow decay of vegetation, both earth and water teemed with animal and vegetable life: thus accounting, at the period of the Deluge, for the vast masses of sea-shells, and for the vast masses of trees which covered the dry portions of the earth, and which were torn up by the Deluge—since converted into coal, embedded at great depths in the earth, in thick seams of pure vegetable matter, without any admixture of mud in the seams, each seam showing the settling in water at *one* time of a great mass of trees.

The mud (since converted into slatey rock), carried by rivers into the ocean depths in the early ages of Adam, was deposited, without carrying any dead remains of once living creatures, none being found in that now rocky Adamite mud, very few creatures having died. As Adam increased in years, other more recently deposited mud, now rocky matter, begins to show a few remains of once animal and vegetable life, these signs increasing as the round earth becomes older. Then *suddenly* comes the vast heaps of transported earthy matter over all the habitable globe, and vast masses of trees, since converted into coal, intermingled with remains of drowned creatures, brought from distant countries, and from the depths of the sea by the great Deluge, in a series of strata—series upon series, all bearing the same stamp, all showing the clearest signs of having been deposited while the round earth was covered with a great depth of water.

The sudden sinkings, which, oh man! thou seest in the thick strata of sandstone, chalk, and coal, are also silent witnesses that the whole of the vast masses of transported matter deposited by the Deluge, settled down, while *all* were in a wet state, upon Adamite and granitic uneven rocks: then, as the waters left the upper portion dry, they became consolidated, the water was driven out, and the consolidated mass sank into the rocky gulfs—sudden gulfs producing the sudden sinkings which, oh man! thou seest.

Moses also records that the Israelitish nation was descended from the holy man Abraham, who was born about 290 years after the deluge, while Noah was yet alive. Abraham had one son Isaac, who had a son Jacob. Jacob had twelve sons, from whom are descended the twelve tribes of Israel. Those twelve sons with their wives settled in the land of Egypt, in the most pleasant and fruitful part of all Egypt, where they multiplied and prospered greatly, they and their descendants, whereupon the Egyptians became envious and compelled them to become slaves, treating them harshly, increasing in severity until it became intolerable. The Israelites prayed earnestly to God to deliver them from their oppressors. God heard their prayers, made Himself known to Moses, a pious Israelite, and appointed him His messenger to the Israelites;—the Israelites had then been located in Egypt more than 400 years, and numbered several hundred thousand men, women, and children. God promised to deliver the Israelites, through Moses, out of the hands of the Egyptians. God commanded Moses to go to Pharaoh the king of Egypt, and demand the liberation of the Israelites from slavery, with permission to depart out of Egypt. Moses did according to what God commanded him to do, and showed his credentials as the true messenger of God, by performing wondrous miracles before Pharaoh, causing Pharaoh to believe in his divine mission, so that he dared not attempt to injure Moses, but heard what he had to say: Pharaoh hesitated, and then refused to part with his Israelitish slaves; thereupon God sent certain plagues which smote the cattle and the people throughout the land of Egypt, sparing only the Israelites, so that the Egyptians being convinced that it was God who was destroying the Egyptians on behalf of the Israelitish slaves, urgently entreated Pharaoh to liberate the Israelites from captivity, and let them depart out of Egypt.

Moses, by command of God, had prepared the Israelites for their departure on a certain night, and commanded them to eat certain things in a certain manner, every family by itself, and called this feast the Feast of the Passover, because God had caused the plagues wherewith He had smitten the Egyptians to pass over the Israelites without hurting them.

Immediately after this feast the Israelites were congregated together, all the men, women, and children, with their herds and flocks, and marched to go out of Egypt. After a little time Pharaoh repented that he had given his consent to let the Israelites go out of Egypt, and hastily collecting an army pursued after the escaping Israelites. God caused a thick mist to intervene between the Israelites and their pursuers, and upon the arrival of the Israelites on the borders of the Red Sea, a sea several tens of miles in width, which formed part of the boundary of Egypt, He caused the Red Sea to open before the Israelites and form a dry channel across from one side to the other, and God commanded Moses to lead them across from one side to the other, enjoining them to be without fear, for God—the creator of all things, who kept the sun, the moon, the earth, and stars in their proper places, their guide and protector—was with them to deliver them out of the hands of the Egyptians. The Israelites journeyed safely across, and the dry channel was purposely left open by God, who foreknew that the Egyptians, in their eager pursuit after the Israelites, would follow them along the dry channel. Moses records that when the whole army of the Egyptians were in the dry channel, pursuing the Israelites, who had got safely across, God suddenly caused the waters to rush back into the channel and drowned the Egyptian army. The Israelites rested in the wilderness, on the side of the Red Sea, opposite to Egypt, and for a while remained there, organizing themselves into a nation, under their prophet Moses ; where God commanded them to remain for forty years. After the death of Moses God appointed Joshua, and at the end of the forty years God commanded him and the Israelites to enter and take possession of the land of Canaan as their national home.

Of the truth of this wonderful narrative the Scriptures teem with the clearest proofs.

That the mighty God—the creator of the wondrous sun, the moon, the earth, and stars—could send the plague to smite the Egyptians, and pass over the Israelites without hurting them, and could cause a thick mist to rise and continue between them and the Egyptians, and could cause the waters of the Red Sea to open so as to form a dry channel across from one side to the other—no man can reasonably doubt; for what are these small things to the constant regular motion of the earth, of the moon, the sun, the planets, and the comets? Surely, He who created them, maintaining them continually in their proper places—He who created all things, could do those small things—things less marvellous than the existence of even one living creature! What proofs have we that God did perform those miracles? There are many proofs, even at this great distance of time, now more than 3000 years.

1. The Holy Scriptures were wholly written by Israelites. The Christian nations of the earth, although hating the Jews for having crucified the Saviour, are constrained to accept as true the Holy Scriptures, for well they know that in no other book has God been revealed. The miracle of the passage of the Israelites across the Red Sea is the most prominent and most frequently mentioned by all the holy writers than any of the other miracles of God.
2. The Israelites have ever since their being thrust out of the land of Egypt been the most remarkable of all the nations of the earth. All the prophets were Israelites; Christ himself was an Israelite; these great facts stamp them as having been the holiest of all the nations in the earth. Their laws and observances were derived through Moses; no other nation has been so wise in understanding the existence of God; no other nation has been so free from idolatry.
3. Their thorough belief in Moses; a belief derived not

merely from Moses, but also through the testimony of the many hundreds of thousands who journeyed with Moses, dryshod, with their flocks and herds, through the dry bed of the Red Sea; which testimony was handed down from father to son, so that the Israelites are constrained to believe in the truthfulness of the miracle.

4. The holiness and truthfulness of Moses and of the written record of Joshua, who also himself passed through the Red Sea dryshod, with Moses and the host of the Israelites; also the truthfulness of their successors, who in their writings give the testimony of other witnesses of the miracle.

5. The prominence given to the miracle in the writings of the prophets, and by the apostles.

6. The sudden appearance of the Israelites as a free nation in a strange land across the Red Sea—the strangeness of their position, their trials, their difficulties, and their murmurings, being recorded by many historians; and their frequent hankerings to return to Egypt, all demonstrating the suddenness of their freedom.

7. The Israelitish nation has always, since their earliest records as a nation, been composed of twelve tribes, each tribe being descended from one of the twelve sons of Jacob: they had no national record until their escape out of the land of Egypt, because not being free men, but slaves in a country not their own, they had no existence as a nation, therefore no national record.

8. The Israelites escaped to a land which had the Red Sea, which is several twenties of miles in width, between them and Egypt; journeying with their wives and children, their flocks and herds, without leaving one behind in Egypt; testifying that a miracle must have been performed by God, to have enabled so large a host safely to cross the wide waters.

9. Think you, oh man! that the wondrous prophecies of Moses, of Isaiah, and of the other prophets, concerning the advent of Christ, could have been so accurately foretold, except through the intervention of God? Are not those prophecies as wondrous as the formation of a dry channel through the Red Sea? Thou knowest, oh man! thou canst not prophesy, for only holy, good, and truthful worshippers of God are His messengers; therefore Moses must have been holy, good, and a truthful worshipper of God.
10. The celebration yearly of the feast of the passover, from its first celebration in the land of Egypt to the present time by the Israelites.
11. Moses and Joshua did not write those utterances, oh man! for *your* edification, but for the edification of those who *actually* crossed the dry channel, and for the edification of their then *living* sons and daughters, that they might not cease to forget the great fact that God was carrying out towards them the promises He made to their forefathers, Abraham, Isaac, and Jacob, and thereby urged them to live holily in the sight of the unseen God, their preserver and guide.
12. The testimony of Christ.

The Holy Scriptures also record that the idolatrous enemies of the Israelites sought to destroy them after the death of Moses, but that the Lord God caused a great storm to arise, and rain great hailstones upon the army of their enemies, destroying many and causing the rest to flee in disorder away from the Israelites, who seeing their flight, and desiring to take advantage of it, Joshua, their holy commander ascended a hill and prayed to God that He would cause the clouds to pass away from over the land, that the sun might shine, and the moon also when the sun had set, that the Israelites might see to follow up their godless persecutors: and the sun instantly shone forth, and afterwards the moon, unobscured by clouds, and the Israelites pursued them throughout that day and throughout that night, so that they were utterly destroyed.

The Israelites were astonished because of the cessation of the storm of hail, of the dreaded thunder, and of the dreaded lightening, for they were eye-witnesses of the rapid change and dispersion of the clouds, while the hands of Joshua were lifted up in prayer; and they were joyous because they thereby knew that God was with Joshua, as he had been with Moses.

Thus were those idolatrous enemies utterly destroyed; for in the sight of God those godless ones were less esteemed than beasts of the field, for in addition to their many other sins, they sought to destroy the true worshippers of God. In this wise the Lord God helped the Israelites, enabling them to possess the land which he had promised Abraham, Isaac, and Jacob their descendants should possess.

Another proof of the truth of the Holy Scriptures is their record of the holy man Abraham, the father of the Jewish people, who was born about 290 years after the deluge. The tombs of Abraham, Sarah his wife, Isaac his son, and of Jacob the son of Isaac, still exist in good preservation, located exactly as described by Moses in Holy Scripture, and which have ever been regarded by the various inhabitants of that land as the tombs of most holy people for about 4000 years.

Another proof is the numerous wonderful prophecies uttered at distant intervals, extending over many hundred years, by those holy men, the prophets, of the coming upon earth of Jesus Christ the Messiah, the deliverer of the souls of men.

Some of these prophecies, notably those of Isaiah, foretell so accurately the whole life and death of Christ, as to have caused multitudes of men erroneously to suppose that they *must* have been written *after* the death of Christ, and not before : and yet Isaiah lived several hundred years before the birth of Christ, and it was these prophecies which led the Jews to look so anxiously for the coming of the Messiah.

The prophets foretold the coming upon earth at an appointed time of an angel—Jesus Christ, the long promised deliverer of the souls of men, the *servant* of the Most High God—from heaven, where He had dwelt with the other angels of God, before the sun, the moon, the stars, and this round earth were made—upon a special mission from God in furtherance of the great plan of God for the salvation of the souls of men—Who should be born into the world as an infant boy, and growing into manhood should live as by far the holiest of men among men for a certain time, and then be ignominiously slain as a malefactor upon a cross;—accurately describing His mother as a pure virgin, and therefore that His birth should be miraculous;—and the time and manner of His birth so truly, that the Jewish nation looked eagerly at the very day and hour that Christ was born, now 1868 years ago, for His birth, as *their* earthly king and deliverer from the Roman bondage, causing by their eagerness so much anxiety to Herod, their cruel king, that he issued a decree for all the young children to be slain that were in Bethlehem—the foretold birthplace of the promised Messiah,—hoping that the infant Messiah might be slain.

The prophets also accurately foretold His holiness of life and wise teachings, the obstacles He should encounter, His betrayal, the price of His betrayal, the potters' field bought with the price, His condemnation to death, the mode by which His peculiar garments should be distributed among His murderers, His crucifixion as a malefactor, the thrust of a spear into His side while on the cross, the prophecy that none of His bones should be broken,—although it was customary to break the legs of all who should die upon the cross,—His burial and resurrection to life on the third day after His death :—all these things being accurately foretold many hundred years before they occurred, by many prophets at various periods.

What greater proofs can we have of the wisdom of God being present in the Scriptures? It is as clearly shown there as in the starry firmament. Every prophecy relating to Christ while on earth having been fulfilled, not one remaining unfulfilled, to cause the least doubt.

That He really was the Messiah, the long promised deliverer of the souls of men, He further proved by the numerous miracles the Holy Spirit of God worked—the Messiah wishing to show to men of His time, and through witnesses to after generations, that He was truly the long promised Messiah.

It was not the purpose of God to show such miracles on behalf of Christ as would compel the Jews to believe in Him, for then they would not have slain Him; therefore Christ ever spoke to them in riddles, because it was *necessary* that Christ should be *slain*, in order that God might pardon the souls of men; therefore, oh man! only just sufficient proofs of Christ being the true Messiah were shown. To all other men those proofs would have been convincing—they would have loved the gentle loving, holy Messiah, and not have slain Him; therefore God waited about 4000 years, for the time when men should exist so blinded by their false traditions, and enraged as to shut their eyes and ears to the sayings and doings of the Messiah, and finally ignominiously to slay Him upon a cross as a malefactor.

That He was more than the sons of Adam, the twelve apostles by their writings are witnesses; they were constrained to believe in Him; the holiness of their lives, their sufferings at the hands of wicked men, prove their firm belief; suffering persecution, stripes, and cruel death; suffering these, because they could not disbelieve the evidence of their eyes, the evidence of their minds, and the evidence of their immortal souls, that the Lord Jesus Christ was truly the long promised Messiah of God.

CHAPTER IX.

Is it Impossible for God to have Communicated with Man?

BEHOLD with thine eyes a MAN—that being upon whom God has showered his inexhaustible love!—him God has endowed with intelligence vastly higher than is possessed by any other living creature? From generation to generation knowledge is handed down—the precepts of the fathers are handed down to the sons, so that in worldly knowledge the sons become wiser than their fathers. The laws of God, by which He governs the earth, are little by little discovered, each generation handing down increased knowledge to its sons; whereas the knowledge possessed by every other living creature, what it is to-day was at the beginning, in the days of Adam; nevertheless, even in those days man was lord over every living creature. Man alone progresses in worldly knowledge—alone has the power of communicating his experience; but for him, note well my friend, the platinum, the gold, the silver, the iron, the lead, the tin, the coal, and the precious stones would have been made in vain,—for he alone of all living creatures has learnt their use, and uses them; he alone of all living creatures is lord of the earth; to him alone has been given the intelligence to subdue all other living creatures to his service, and causing those to multiply which are serviceable to him; to man alone the earth becomes increasingly fruitful,—he alone sows that the earth may bring forth its increase.

Thus man is lord of the whole round earth; from its inner parts he gets his metals, his coal, his building stone, and brick; from the surface it yields up its increase; things animate and inanimate he bends to his service.

Do you not thus perceive, my friend, an unity of design throughout creation,—that all things which exist in the starry skies exist in accordance with a settled plan—a simple plan—perfect from the very first? Meditate a little: the inanimate sun, the first of all created things, vivifies and gives light to numberless stars, to the moon, and this round earth; it is the only source whence they obtain light, in like manner as a lighted candle is the only source of light in an otherwise dark room. The moon reflects light from the burning sun, while moving around the earth, reflecting upon the round earth the sun's light somewhere every night—reflecting it in like manner as silvered glass reflects the light of a candle; winds, ocean-tides, and clouds are produced, all absolutely necessary to life, as absolutely necessary as food; the pleasant changes of day and night, every twenty-four hours; of summer and autumn, winter and spring, every year—the one succeeding the other with the utmost order, from generation to generation; the surface of the round earth teeming with vegetation and with living creatures, in numberless variety, no two living things being exactly alike, therein exhibiting the illimitable wisdom and creative power of God,—for every one of the numberless germs in every living vegetation and in every one of the living creatures that were made on the sixth day of creation was also dissimilar the one to the other. And upon the round earth stands man—the last created and most important of all created things—of all the things therein vastly pre-eminent—pre-eminent, because he has a soul, that holy, heavenly thing, which places a great gulf between him and the gorilla, that living creature which, of all living creatures, is outwardly most like him; then, by almost inappreciable degrees, living creatures are seen less and less like him, until all similarity is lost in that which, like a stone, never had the semblance of life within it.

Now friend, see you not in all these things unity of design,— that God has a fixed plan, and that all the things He made during the first six days were made for the comfort and happiness of man while living upon the round earth,—and that upon him God has showered, with inexhaustible love, His goodness? And cannot you comprehend, oh man! that God, as part of His great unalterable plan, has provided a far happier dwelling in the illimitable heavens which surround the starry skies, for those of mankind who have the sense to worship Him—the highest of all sense,—God assisting them successfully to pass the ordeal required for promotion, by giving as their guide the Holy Scriptures,—for none who have not this sense can be promoted into heaven,—like as the spiritually senseless brutes cannot gain entrance therein.

Now say, do you not think, my friend, that God would make Himself known to man whom he loves so well? for whom He has created the round earth and all that is therein, and sun, and moon, and stars; and whom He has endowed with capacity to understand His will? Do you not think that God can communicate with man, and man with God?

All these things the Holy Scriptures record that God has done; they record His laws, His plan of redemption, and the way it has been and is being carried out.

CHAPTER X.

The Great Wisdom Revealed in the Scriptures.

THE crowning proof of the truth of the Holy Scriptures, is their unapproachable wisdom throughout. Those who have studied them the most, even having studied them to find flaws, are just those who value them the most highly, esteeming all other books as mere trash in comparison, for none other will bear searching investigation; no one part contradicting another, but all throughout giving proofs innumerable that every part was revealed by God Himself.

Common sense, therefore, must, of necessity, come to the conclusion that the Holy Scriptures give a truthful and reasonable account of the existence of God, and his reasons for creating man.

CHAPTER XI.

The Common Sense of the Holy Scriptures.

HOW incomparable appear the truths as revealed in the Holy Scriptures—truths that are stamped with the highest wisdom—by the side of the silly inventions and fables of man, and which insult the common sense of mankind! Compare them with the Papal lies—which teach the worship of reputed saints, the worship of a woman, the use of images and pictures in worship, ignoring altogether the commandment of God, "Thou shalt not make to thyself any graven image, to bow down before it, or to reverence it, for I am the Lord thy God." Images and pictures of idolaters foolishly represent the all-powerful, ever-present, unseen, living God, the creator of the starry heavens and earth, as a man having a head and body, legs fingers and toes, like a gorilla,—both images and pictures made by man, no two alike, and stupidly worshipped as representing God.

Impostor priests have set up in various parts of this round earth images and pictures of a man upon a cross, and of a woman with a child in her arms, in thousands distributed about the earth. They teach the young and foolish to look fondly upon them as holy and *necessary* things, and sometimes teach them to believe that the mighty God is bodily in the plaster, wood, and stone composing the images, even leading the more crazy to believe that he can see the lips of the image or picture move, and wink its eyes. Some of the more cunning and impious priests teaching their crazy followers that to touch their images is to touch the holy Person of God, or of the Virgin Mary, whom they impiously style the Queen of Heaven, and thereby be healed of disease. They have even with great pomp and ceremony at the present day, like the competition among professionals and traders, *crowned* an exceptional image and pay it adoration, as though it were alive—the idiotic people ready and willing in their blindness to believe the senseless trash the cunning impious priests say, but ignoring the Scriptures.

Thou canst, oh man! quickly distinguish the carved, dumb, inanimate images, the work of men's hands, from the living creatures, the handiwork of God. Exercise also thy common sense in spiritual matters, and learn to distinguish the great wisdom of the Scriptures from the superstition and fables of spurious churches.

CHAPTER XII.

Disbelievers in God as it were Human Wolves.

OF all men there are none so senseless as atheists: of all men they are most like the spiritually senseless brutes in their thoughts and actions: they even surpass in folly the foolish idolators. It is belief in the existence of God that civilizes man by restraining his animal propensities; without that restraint disbelievers in God are those persecutors of mankind, liars, thieves, fornicators, adulterers, those filthy animals harlots, and murderers; and among uncivilized men are cannibals, who, like wolves, slay and eat the flesh of their own kind.

CHAPTER XIII.

YOU thus, my friend, perceive that there is a great unseen Being in existence whom men call God; that He has communicated with man, and that the Holy Scriptures are the revelation of God to man. God has given us innumerable proofs of His existence in the mountains, the hills, the valleys, in the starry skies, in the air, in the waters, in the ground, and in living creatures,—all being the handiwork of God. The houses, the ships, and the various contrivances of man are shaped by man out of things which were previously made through the instrumentality of God,—man simply shapes them. It is necessary, my friend, that every one of us should convince ourselves that God exists, although we cannot see Him, so that having this sure foundation we may fervently worship Him.

Remember, oh my brother! and you, oh my sister! that thou hast had life within thee for about 6000 years—first asleep in Adam, and afterwards asleep in thy fathers. Like as mummy wheat that has been wrapped in mummy cloths for 3000 years, waited 3000 years to be planted in the ground, then sprouted into a plant, so did the living sleeping germs that were in Adam wait for about 6000 years for thy birth into the world as *separate* beings.

God graciously created thee and placed thee in Adam for a high and mighty purpose, having great love for thee. He strongly yearns towards thee, desiring that thou mightest live in the illimitable heavens which surround the starry skies, with His holy angels, and be as His holy angels for ever. Thy *birth* into the world is but a new phase in thy existence; the Holy God then commenced to test *thy* souls in like manner as He tested the soul of Adam. The individual souls of all that have died have been tried whether in the sight of God they were priceless, or worthless as dross; and now it is *thy* turn, if thou art found, when thou diest, to be a true, worshipping, pardoned soul, thou wilt be priceless in the sight of God; but if not, then thy soul will be as worthless dross. Upon thyself, and thyself alone, oh my brother! and you, oh my sister! hangs the judgment. Believe in God and worship Him, and then through the mediatory death of His holy Son, our Redeemer, thou wilt be priceless. God and His glorious Son plead to thee their yearning love for thee, and place before thy mental eyes the great happiness they have for ever for thee in the joyous holy heavens; reciprocate their love, and upon thy knees quickly ask, while thou art yet alive, for forgiveness of thy sins, and thy sins will be forgiven thee; continue steadfast in the right way, and when thou diest thou wilt be numbered among the priceless ones.

CHRIST IS COMING.

PART II.

THE HOLY SCRIPTURES

AND THEIR

DESCRIPTION OF THE MIGHTY PLAN OF GOD.

CHAPTER I.

Spurious Traditions.

YE have read, oh ye nations, that the Creator of all things is really and truly a living Being, whom men call God, that He has revealed himself to man, and that the Holy Scriptures are the only true revelations of His holy precepts, revealed through His instrumentality, that they might be sure guides to mankind, whereby they might be truly taught what constituted goodness in the sight of God and what constituted evil.

Now, oh ye nations of every land, look well into your other books which you call sacred, and compare them with the Holy Scriptures of God, and ye will find them utterly at variance and full of superstitious nonsense, deceiving you, instilling into you spurious notions of the one holy God, and of His holy precepts. Be wise now, and let every willing nation form a council, one council representing all the nations of the world out of its most learned laymen—the Jew, the professed Christian, and those of every other people—and let them investigate thoroughly and dispassionately their supposed sacred books, and compare them with the Holy Scriptures, and let them judge whether their supposed sacred books are true and inspired, or whether they be untrue or uninspired, and your mental eyes will be opened, and you will become truly wise, discerning that your supposed sacred books were written after the promulgation of many portions of the Holy Scriptures, and that the portions which are really good and sensible were borrowed from the Holy Scriptures, and the rest simply the absurd notions of foolish men, be assured that the sect who refuses to have its doctrines tested by the one great test of the Holy Scriptures—by the common-sense spirit of the Holy Scriptures alone—has fears that its peculiar doctrines are untrue; for like as a liar is fearful of having his lies inquired into, so is that sect; nevertheless, whether a sect refuses or assents, test its doctrines—test the doctrines of every sect, and sternly let your council give judgment, giving clear reasons for its judgment, as in the sight of God.

Consider the idolatrous nations of old; they ignorantly thought they worshipped God, each having different ceremonials; each its own set of idols; its own set of spurious priests; reverencing them as you reverence your spurious priests; its own set of absurd traditions; each led by its priests and deceived by them; each so firmly believing—as firmly as yourselves—that the most devout willingly encountered death in behalf of their religion, some willingly putting themselves to great torment and to many privations. Nevertheless, God abhorred them, for their worship was sham and spurious, for they ignorantly preferred to follow the imagination of their foolish priests than seek the real precepts of God in the Holy Scriptures. They worshipped a lie, even becoming fond of the lic; therefore God abhorred them. Examine their mythology and, behold, their supposed worship was not true worship but rank folly, and their traditions mere fables, concocted not by the people, but by the spurious priests for the purpose of holding them in spiritual bondage. Ah, you comprehend the folly of *their* worship, the absurdity of *their* ceremonials, and the nonsense of *their* mythology. Thou canst see they were foolish, very thoughtless, and very void of common sense, because *their* spurious priests had imbibed from youth the nonsense of their elders and thereby became very foolish, very thoughtless, and void of common sense, and therefore taught their people to be like themselves. Such as those nations were, oh ye people of every land, *so are you.* There is not a righteous nation in the whole world, no not one ; nay, more, in no nation are there many righteous ; there are but few who truly comprehend the one God of the Holy Scriptures ; there are but few who possess spiritual common sense ; there are but few whom spurious ministers have not deceived. Therefore, mankind are split into many sects ; like as sometimes a pitiable idiot believes himself to be a king, so do some of the pitiable clericals believe themselves to be more than ordinary men, as special messengers from God; deceiving themselves and their pitiable people ; the idiot, the minister, and the people alike pitiably deceived, deceiving one another.

The spurious Churches of the worshippers of the sun, the worshippers of the cow, of the monkey, of the serpent, and the many worshippers of imaginary Gods, and the Papacy, have stood for so many generations, not because their doctrines were true, but because God has not interfered with them in like manner that He interferes not with the murderer. God has deemed it a necessity that mankind should possess free-will. He has limited himself in giving them only His advice. He turns no man to the right hand nor to the left, neither to do a good thing nor to do evil; in no other way than through the Holy Scriptures does God influence the ways of men. The good things which men do are done directly or indirectly through the advice given in His holy word, but the evil things which men do are done through their wilful ignorance of the teachings of God, and through their forgetfulness of Him. God has given to every man the tremendous power to obey or disobey Him, a power which none other of His creatures have. On the other hand, God reserves to Himself the right of carrying into Heaven the obedient and shutting out from Heaven for ever the disobedient.

Ponder over these awful words, oh ye nations, and look keenly into your suppposed sacred books, and ye will find them full of rottenness and full of sham. Behold the time is at hand, even knocking at the door, when the axe of scriptural truth will be laid at the root of the many spiritual errors, and they will be cut down. And the thoughtful in every nation will become wise, having their spiritual eyes opened, and they will band themselves together, the Jew and the Gentile, resolutely succouring each other as men of one mind. And they will teach the people around them scriptural truths, and the people will comprehend them, and all the nations will be of one mind, every nation as it were an independent branch, their root and their stem being Christ, their common bond, whose dwelling-place is with God his Father, in heaven.

See to it, ye nations, that *every* child be taught aright, and shield your people with a stern hand from deceitful teachers; remembering that erroneous teachings in early life usually blind the judgment during life, so that the youthful idolator usually dies an idolator; the youthful sectarian usually dies a sectarian; and the youthful papist usually dies a papist. As the child is taught, that he usually retains till death; therefore, ye nations, see to it that every child is taught aright. Be not credulous, but prove all things.

CHAPTER II.

BE not credulous concerning spiritual things, neither be short sighted, but prove all things by the light of common sense. In worldly matters your judgment is keen; be as sensible in things that are spiritual. Remember always that too ready belief is the nurse of general superstition, of spiritual nonsense, and of individual superstition, and that on the other hand a mulish determination to disbelieve, or a supercilious captiousness, is the nurse of all that is vile in man.

First convince yourselves that God really exists—the things your eyes behold will give you innumerable proofs—then, ye nations, convince yourselves that the Holy Scriptures were inspired by God—they give you many proofs—there is no book comparable to it in wisdom, no other book that so widely separates good from evil, yet no other book so ancient, no other book that is free from untruth and imaginative theories, no other book that bears the impress of God, in its description of the creation, of the starry skies and the round earth, in the purpose for which man was created, in the description of the deluge, in the formation of the Israelitish nation, in the prophecies, in the real miracles and in spiritual morality; so that having faith, oh ye nations, in the existence of the living God, and in the inspiration of the Holy Scriptures, you cause His Holy Word to be the *one* test of all spiritual things, yourselves judging whether they accord or disaccord with the Holy Word of God; yourselves sternly destroying the spiritual books that are proved to be the works of imaginative men. Put not any faith in the writings of uninspired men, in men who have lived upon earth since the days of the last of the twelve apostles of the Messiah, nor be credulous in things that are incomprehensible; for a doctrine that is inexplicable, that is incomprehensible to common-sense, bears upon it the stamp of untruth; inasmuch as every *real* doctrine is explained many times in the Holy Word. Therefore understand, ye nations, let these words sink deeply into your souls; a doctrine that is not plainly comprehensible, that is not plainly explicable, satisfactorily to the common-sense of the intelligent among mankind, or that is explained in a way contrary to the spirit of wisdom, and of the common-sense which pervades the Holy Scriptures, is utterly unworthy of belief, bearing on the face of it the stamp of untruth.

And remember, ye nations, the things of nature are infinitely more wonderful than the imaginative thoughts of men; therefore eschew and sternly prohibit the production of books containing fairy tales and other far-fetched foolish tales of the imagination, for they lead the mind to rest upon superstitious nonsense. Spiritual truth bears upon its front plainly, without mystery, the stamp of truth; the more it is intelligently investigated the more numerous are its evidences. Contrariwise, spiritual untruth bears upon its front the stamp of mystery, of inexplication and nonsense, the more it is intelligently investigated; therefore, ye nations, close resolutely the mouth of spiritual liars, those evil spirits which wrap around them the garb of holiness that they might the more easily deceive the souls of men. Try your teachers of spiritual things frequently, whether they be true teachers or teachers of spiritual lies to the people. If one should openly declare that himself or his coadjutors possess spiritual power more than ordinary men, or that bread or wine are converted into other substances by them, demand of him his proofs; if he withholds those proofs, or if his bread and wine have the ordinary appearance of bread and wine, set him sternly down as a liar, and suffer him to be no longer a teacher of the people. If anyone should impiously say that himself or his coadjutors are empowered to forgive sins, ask him to show by some miracle that he has warranty for his statement. Be not deceived, nor foolishly lenient, nor superstitious, for it is a sign of a spurious priest that he is a mere pretender; pretending to do things which he is really unable to do. If he cannot show a sign satisfactorily to the common sense above other ordinary men, consider him a wilful deceiver; therefore, unworthy to be a teacher of the people. Or if one is a user of images or of pictures in his worship of God, demand of him why he contravenes the commandment of God, if he cannot produce a greater authority for so doing than the words of uninspired men, unmentioned in the Scriptures, set him also sternly down as a deceiver of himself and a snare to the superstitiously inclined, and suffer him no longer to be a teacher of the people, nor permit those unworthy men to officiate in the sanctuaries, for they are abhorrent to God because they are liars. Neither permit them to hold any office of trust or authority; let them be considered as men evil minded, like to the violent, the fraudulent, and the abominable. As you would repress them, so repress those who lie concerning things that are spiritual, be neither weak nor irresolute, nor in the least superstitious, but repress them firmly; chronicle neither their sayings nor their doings; let common sense, the intelligence common to all men whose thoughts are not warped by nonsense, guide you in your judgment; let truth alone guide you.

Be sternly matter-of-fact, give credence to what is true, but abhor that which is untrue; then will the nations no longer be discordant one with the other, no longer split into many sects, for, being followers of truth, they will become loving brethren of one family and chase from their midst as they arise the fables that cause disunion and unhappiness throughout the earth.

CHAPTER III.

Sacred Things.

BE not, oh ye nations, superstitious about things which foolish men deem sacred, but discriminate between things which are truly sacred and those which are not sacred.

All things which are good are sacred, but things that are evil are not sacred; truth is sacred, but untruth is not sacred; the Holy Scriptures are sacred because they were inspired by God, but written words and sayings not inspired by God are not sacred. The true worshippers of God are sacred in His sight, because they are His adopted children; but those who are not true worshippers are not sacred, for they are not His children; the ordinances of God are sacred, because they emanate from Him for the guidance of men, but the ordinances of men are not sacred because they are not prompted by God; the sanctuaries wherein men worship in accordance with the Holy Scriptures, and all within them, are sacred, because they are set aside by men for the true worship of God; things which are merely old are not sacred, for disobedience to God is not sacred; all things which are in accordance with the Holy Scriptures are sacred, because they are in accordance, but nought which is not in accordance is sacred. And there are degrees of sacredness; for those who truly minister in the services of God, and those who truly teach the people their duty to God, are more sacred than those who do not do those things. The life of mankind is ordained by God to be held sacred by man, whether a man be good or evil, but the life of a good man is to be accounted more sacred than the life of an evil man; in the sight of God the life of a good man is sacred, but the life of an evil man is not sacred.

The life of a good ruler, and those having authority that are good, are like the true minister and the true teacher, sacred in the sight of God, because by their good example they incline the people to do well; but an evil ruler and evil men who are in authority are not sacred but abhorrent in the sight of God, more so than other men, and men should resolutely refuse to have evil men in any post of authority over them, or to obey them, for evil men in authority, by their evil example, are the cause, indirectly, of much misery in the world, and the cause of the loss of many souls; therefore they are as a curse upon the people and utterly abhorrent to God. The sacredness of a man in the sight of God is in proportion to the good he does to his own soul, and to the souls of the children of men. No one thing that is inanimate is more sacred than any other like thing, for all are equal, able neither to do an evil thing nor do a good thing; but the inanimate things which form the true sanctuaries of God, wherein the people truly worship, and all the necessary things within them, are sacred, in that they are dedicated to the religious services of God by those who take the Holy Scriptures as their only guide : therefore, wilfully to injure them or to steal them is an offence in the sight of God that is very heinous, being an injury to Himself, also to His own adopted children.

The true Church is sacred in the sight of God because the worshippers are His adopted children, but the spurious Churches are not sacred because, being founded in error, the worshippers are not His children. A nation wherein all the people are pure worshippers of God would be a sacred nation, for all would then be the adopted children of God, therefore holy in His sight; hereafter in God's appointed time it will be so. The holiness of a nation depends upon a right knowledge of spiritual things, and its degree of zeal in carrying out the principles of that knowledge in earthly things as well as in spiritual things. In like manner as the nations of the whole world have become unholy through their wilful carelessness of what is right and what wrong, thereby causing an unwillingness in the people to restrain their own brutish passions, so they will become holy through right knowledge, and by each person resolutely repressing all tendencies to do evil; repressing his own brutish tendencies and the brutish tendencies of others.

The cross is not sacred in the sight of God, because, like the scourge, it was a vile instrument in the hands of the murderers of the Messiah; it is rather an emblem of the vileness of man— a thing not glorious to man, but to cause man to weep and abhor it in very shame.

CHAPTER IV

The Duty of the Nations.

TAKE heed that the young be taught aright in accordance with the spirit of the Holy Scriptures; let your laws be plain, few, and simply carried out; give the well-disposed perfect liberty, but sternly repress the evil-disposed; sternly repressing the domination of foreign priests, directly or indirectly, over you, ignore them utterly within your own boundaries; repress sternly the liar, the dishonest, the thief, the violent, the drunkard, the stirrer-up of strife, the fornicator, and the grasping rich, that the well-disposed may live in peace, and that the laborious may not be as slaves to the rich; remembering that the well-disposed are willing to obey good laws, but the evil are by their evil habits disposed to break the laws of God and man. And ye rulers take especial heed that yourselves obey the laws, for as ye obey so will the people; remembering that many laws are a sign that the nation is wrongly governed—governed more in accordance with the foolish maxims of men, rather than by the wise precepts of God; let evil in all things be chained and sternly repressed, not with cruelty nor by the shedding of blood, but with firmness of purpose.

Suffer no person to be a teacher of the people who is defective in a knowledge of the spirit of the Holy Scriptures; nor suffer any teacher to lie by pretending to the people that his appointment is from God or from His glorious Son, for such pretenders lie to elevate themselves in the estimation of the people. God neither appoints the teachers of the people, nor murderers to murder the people. Take heed that all appointed by the State to carry out the laws and duties intrusted by the nation do their duty, not carelessly but thoroughly, as in the sight of God, being strictly subordinate each to those in higher authority, that the government of a nation may be strong and moved as one man, having one mind, not striving one against the other, but all in one direction, towards the mighty God their Creator, and His glorious Son our Redeemer and King.

Let all the nations who love righteousness, and peace, and justice between man and man, band themselves firmly together, recognising each other as brethren under the leadership of one King, their Redeemer Christ, and resolutely repress the evil passions within their nations; let all those nations be united and move together towards their King in Heaven as one man, so that if one suffers all suffer, if one resists the aggression of evil nations all resist—resisting not for the sake of vanity or for ambition, or hatred or love of strife, or for selfishness, but that the people, within the boundaries of the peaceably-disposed nations, may rest in peace and quietness—resisting only to drive out the aggressive foreigner within the boundaries of any of the united nations—resisting with all their might; and with none other let them form alliances.

CHAPTER V.

Holy Ghost.

IN Heaven there are many holy spirits—God, His glorious Son, and innumerably happy angels—these are all spirits, in that they have neither flesh nor blood; yet they are alive, and they are all holy. Scripture calls only *one* of those holy spirits by the name of Holy Ghost, that *one* Holy Spirit being God—He being the holiest and chief of all, the mainspring of all. Holy Ghost is one of the names of the *one* God; in like manner as God is sometimes called Holy Father.

The Holy Person of God is in the Heaven of Heavens, the dwelling-place of God; but the living cloud is everywhere throughout space; the Holy Person and the living cloud constituting one Holy God. That living cloud Scripture sometimes designates as the Holy Spirit of God, and sometimes the Holy Ghost, both being names of the *one* only God. The Holy Spirit of God, the living cloud which is everywhere throughout all space, shrinks to great tenuity from the person of a wicked man, abhorring him; but when that man, becoming convinced of the nonsense of his past thoughts and actions, repents his folly and becomes a sincere follower of Christ, then the holy living cloud no longer shrinks from him, but enters lovingly into him, continuing there, thereby sanctifying him, that is, stamping him with God's stamp of holiness in the sight of God—stamping him as veritably a saved soul and an accepted child of God—God being then in him and he in God.

Sometimes Scripture designates as the Holy Ghost the utterances of God, because they are part of the mind of God. The prophets were moved by the Holy Ghost, and were full of the Holy Ghost, because having much knowledge of those utterances of God—the Holy Scriptures—what they said and did were actuated by those Scriptures, and sometimes they were prompted by the Holy Spirit, the living cloud, to reveal new tidings.

Sometimes the Holy Spirit of God is called the Spirit of Truth, because God, having a perfect knowledge of all things and hating lies, is pre-eminently the primal source of all truth— is truth itself; and so are His utterances, the Holy Scriptures: they are the spirit of truth, truth as it were embodied in the relations of man to God, capable of being read by the eyes of man, but not by the eyes of any other living creature on the face of the earth. In like manner as the sun is the source of all the light our eyes can see, so the Holy Scriptures are the source (primarily derived from God) of our knowledge of God; they are the fountain of all the right knowledge mankind possess; they are holy emanations from the holy mind of God. By means of the Scriptures God guides the truly wise of mankind to heaven, and they are as necessary to man in obtaining an everlasting home in heaven as the Messiah himself; therefore it was that the holy Messiah commanded his ministers to preach the glad tidings to the nations, and baptise them in the name of the Father, of the Son, and of the Holy Ghost—the Scriptures—because all three are absolutely necessary to the salvation of the souls of men, and God has ordained all three to be an equal necessity to man.

1. God as the Creator.
2. Christ as the Ransom.
3. The Holy Scriptures—the mind of God—ever present in the world, teaching us the way to heaven.

These three :—
1. The Holy God,
2. The Holy Messiah,
3. The Holy Scriptures,

are the three great and mighty witnesses bearing record, all agreeing in the great fact that Christ is veritably the Messiah of God; the Scriptures foretelling long beforehand when and how the Messiah should come, and witnessing that he really came as foretold.

These things have been hidden from you, oh ye nations of the whole earth, because the follies of your predecessors have made you as foolish as themselves in all things that are spiritual, so that ye have only a misty notion of God; part of the nations have altogether forgotten the Scriptures, and some have taken to themselves the foolish doctrine of a *trinity* of *persons*, as constituting *one* 'God, in like manner as some nations have foolishly taken to themselves the worship of images and pictures; a doctrine utterly at variance with the whole of the Scripture, a doctrine utterly unknown to all the holy men mentioned in the Scriptures, a doctrine unmentioned in the Scriptures, a doctrine inexplicable satisfactorily to the common-sense of Holy Scripture, because it is a lie, as untrue as some of the other doctrines of the many spurious churches.

Now understand, oh ye foolish nations, the Messiah Christ is the only *born* son of the mighty God, the creator of all things, for whom the mighty God made the starry skies, this round earth, and all that are therein; the only angel of God that has been born into the world, born that as man he might by the *perfect* holiness of his life, while living upon the earth, be a pure and an acceptable atonement for the great sin of Adam, which was the introduction of disobedience towards God into the world. In striving to prove Christ to be the one God, men perforce mystify themselves and say nonsense; like those who strive to make what is really untrue appear to be true.

Nonsense has swayed the nations of the world, and they have almost forgotten the God of Truth, the creator of all things; for, being mystified, they have no pleasure in reading the Holy Scriptures; they have been as a book that is sealed, as a language almost unknown. Spurious churches teach their members that belief in the lying doctrine is *absolutely necessary* in order to enter heaven, thus heaping in their folly an untrue dogma upon a lying doctrine, that mankind might be frightened into belief of the lying doctrine; thus do men build their sects, trusting much to the utterances of their foolish teachers, while trusting only a little to the Word of God.

Of a certainty, oh ye nations, the time is at hand when the Holy Spirit of God will prompt men to burst the chains of nonsense which men have coiled round men, and you will become wise in spiritual things, and a great change will come over the thoughts of the nations; and the utterances of God—the Holy Scriptures—you will cherish, and they will actuate your ways, yourselves restraining yourselves resolutely from evil.

CHAPTER VI.

The one Foundation-Theme of the Holy Scriptures.

THE one theme upon which the Holy Scriptures are built are these—

1. The unity of the Godhead. God is one holy being, and Christ is another holy being, the one as separate and distinct in person from the other, as a human father is distinct from his son.

2. God being the only source of all good things, the creator and governor of all things, is therefore that almighty wondrous holy being men call God, and whom the Messiah Christ, like unto the children of Adam, calls *his* God. God calling Christ His son and His servant.

3. The unity of the Godhead, Christ not being God, but inferior only to God; God placing him next in authority to Himself; but not until after the resurrection of Christ, for until then God had not promoted him to be next in authority in Heaven to Himself, for until then Christ had not by his mediatory death delivered the souls of worshipping men.

4. God has laid down certain laws for the governance of all things, especially one for His own guidance, which law prohibits Him from carrying into Heaven any living thing that has not upon it the stamp of *perfect* goodness.

5. God made man expressly with the intention of peopling a part of the Holy Heavens with those of mankind who, by their own free will, attain the stamp of *perfect* goodness, while living upon the earth.

6. The one theme proclaims the great fact that mankind acquires that stamp of *perfect* goodness by following the advice of God as revealed in the Holy Scriptures, acquiring it by

restraining the brutish inclinations of their bodies, in comprehending the advice of God—worshipping Him, in sincerely and zealously accepting as their leader and deliverer His glorious son the Christ, and by spiritually loving one another.

7. The promise of God that an angel, their future King in heaven, should come out of heaven and live upon earth as man, who by his perfect holiness should become their Messiah, that is the deliverer of the souls of those who worshipped God.

These good things are the *one* foundation-theme of the Holy Scriptures, of every prophet, and of every holy man mentioned in the Scriptures. They severally in their generations reiterated and impressed upon the thoughtful among their hearers these good things; the later writers of the Holy Scriptures, the Apostles of Christ, teaching that Christ was veritably God's promised angel, the Messiah: proving it by the prophecies, by his miracles, by his own words, by witnessing his resurrection to life after the death of his body upon the cross, and by the testimony of their own eyes, they having beheld his ascension through the air upwards towards heaven.

CHAPTER VII.

THE Holy Scriptures are the only inspired writings in the world; they were written by those holy men, the mouthpieces of God; to them He revealed His advice for the guidance of mankind; and to them He revealed His mighty plan, revealing the great happiness He has in store for those of mankind who have the common sense to follow His advice. Those holy men were God's appointed messengers from Himself to all mankind; in their own words and in their own language they proclaimed the messages of God. The ideas were revealed by God to His messengers, but God left to them the explanation. They were inspired revelations written and uttered by the holy messengers in ordinary uninspired words; like many teachers of one theme, each gave his own explanation of the *one* theme.

The Holy Scriptures are a revelation of the mighty plan of God, from its commencement to the death of the last of the Apostolic eye-witnesses of the victory of the Messiah, the deliverer, over the temptations of the world and the temptations of his body while living as a man upon the earth ; when those eye-witnesses died the Holy Scriptures were completed and nothing has been added thereto that is true.

The Holy Scriptures are also a record of the actions and sayings of holy people from the commencement of creation down to the time of the last of the twelve Apostles of the Messiah, an interval of about 4000 years. Those holy writers were the wisest of all mankind, for they had a more perfect knowledge of God than other men.

It was not the purpose of God to give man a knowledge of things appertaining to the necessities of his body—for that experience would give to man—nor to teach man the intricate laws by which God governs the universe : but the purpose of God was to teach man how to gain immortal life in Heaven—but for the revelations of God man could not possibly know aught about Him. The intelligence the soul gives to man would simply have made men the most cunning and vilest of all created things, like to the godless, causing some to dwindle into savage men, like as many brutes have dwindled into cruel creatures; therefore, oh nations, the Holy Scriptures are inestimable to mankind, and great has been your blindness concerning them.

Every nation of old believed in the existence of one or more gods, through oral traditions that were handed down from Noah, from father to son, from one ignorant foolish man to another, becoming hazier through each descent, ending in a jumble of nonsense throughout every nation, the Jewish nation only excepted, that nation only having a right knowledge of God, derived through the Jewish mouthpieces of God. The Holy Scriptures are the great antidote of God to the brutal tendencies of the flesh and blood of man, they are the ladder by which men reach Heaven.

God has deemed it a necessity that man should not be coerced into worshipping Him. He has deemed it a necessity that man should, by his own free-will, gain entrance into Heaven by the meritorious acts of comprehending God and worshipping Him, supplicating for past misdeeds, through the mediatory death of the holy Messiah, the deliverer ; by these meritorious acts only is man of more value in the sight of God than are the brutes.

In like manner as the starry skies, the wondrous living creatures, the wondrous living vegetation, and the wondrous inanimate things of the earth, appeal to the eyes of man as evidence of the existence of God, so the Holy Scriptures appeal to the soul of man, urging him to worship the unseen God, the Creator of all things, and His Holy Son, the Messiah. The Holy Scriptures teach him concerning things which the eyes cannot see, giving many examples of what constitutes evil and what constitutes goodness in the sight of God, giving many examples of many kinds of good men and many kinds of evil men.

The prophets were spiritual lights of the world, because God caused them to be the revealers of spiritual things, but God Himself was the source of their light. Christ, in Scripture, is significantly called *the* light of the world, because God caused him to reveal to the children of Adam, the great and marvellous fact that he was veritably the Messiah, the deliverer of worshipping men, the ransom appointed by God, before the creation of the starry skies, for the ransoming of the soul of Adam, and that he it was whom God was about to suffer wicked men to slay. It was Christ who largely shed more than any child of Adam the light of true wisdom; therefore he is called in Scripture the light of the world, and his followers are called after his name. In his light, his revelations, they shape their thoughts and deeds; he is their standard, their rallying point, their bond of union, their heavenly friend and guide in obtaining the favour of God; in like manner as the lesser revelations of Moses shaped the thoughts and the deeds of the children of Abraham after their captivity, so the utterances of the holy Messiah shape the thoughts and deeds of his true followers.

CHAPTER VIII.

GOD deemed it indispensable before he commenced the work of creation, that mankind should have perfect free-will—free to follow His holy advice or not to follow it—reserving to Himself the right of rewarding the obedient, by carrying them into heaven, and of punishing the disobedient, by considering them as mere brutes unworthy to enter heaven; therefore He has left to the family of man the safe keeping of His written Word.

The Holy Scriptures having been left wholly in the keeping of the family of man, are liable to be erroneously translated, erroneously interpreted, and erroneously printed; nay, more, even wilfully perverted by impious men, traitors to their fellow-men. To understand the Scriptures aright, they must be read from the beginning to the end, like the reading of other books—reading in the light of common sense, thoughtfully discriminating between the words that apply to the things of earth and the things of heaven; those which apply to the body and those which apply to the soul; remembering that every desire, every intention, and every real doctrine of God is repeated many times, first by one of the holy writers, then by others, sometimes even several times by each. It is therefore unwise and impious to strive to establish a doctrine upon a few ambiguous words, written probably by only one of the holy writers; for such folly has mystified the mighty plan of God, causing it to be incomprehensible to the minds of men, causing them to forget God altogether, through being bewildered, or to lead them to believe in that which is untrue, thereby occasioning disputations, heart burnings, and disunion; so that the ambiguous words have been scatterers of the foolish ones who unwisely cling to the ambiguous rather than to that which is plain, through the folly of their teachers.

Remembering that Satan, sin, evil spirits, are not alive, but signify *active* disobedience—God is the only invisible being in this round earth; there is none other; therefore be not deceived by fables, neither be superstitious. A man writes a book, writing words dictated by his unseen soul. You, my friend, read it; thy unseen soul communes with the past thoughts of his unseen soul, perchance being moved to tears or to laugh or to drink in his evil or his good sayings, as though verily he was talking with thee; so, when thou readest the Holy Scriptures, or do aught in following the holy advice of God, the spirit of the unseen living God, thy loving Father, the great author of the Holy Scriptures, the prompter of His servants, the holy writers, communes with thy soul as though verily He was talking with thee; and verily He watches thy emotions, for the words He uttered to the holy men of old He utters to thee, and the glorious promises he made to them He makes to thee.

And understand, ye nations, that the true Church of God is easily distinguishable from the many spurious Churches, for the Holy Scriptures accepted by the true Church are in strict accordance with common-sense, their wisdom fully satisfies the most intelligent of men; therefore they are the bond of union, because, being true, they are free from nonsense; whereas the scriptural interpretation accepted by some spurious Churches—being mystical, therefore subject to several diverse interpretations—causes division and bitterness; and the adulterated Scriptures of other spurious Churches being revolting to the common-sense of mankind, by reason of their nonsense stamping them as untrue, are brands of discord, breeding wars and perpetuating evil and misery among mankind.

Therefore, ye nations, be wise, suffer not imprudent teachers to bewilder the people with that which is ambiguous or adulterated, but acquaint yourselves with the *one* foundation theme—the spiritual rock upon which the Holy Scriptures are built, that you may rightly understand the true spirit of the whole.

CHAPTER IX.

YOUR common-sense, oh ye nations, would naturally induce you to suppose that as the Holy Scriptures contain proofs innumerable of the highest wisdom, and proofs of having been inspired by God, they would have found their way to the hearts and understanding of all men; but look around you upon the whole of mankind, and mark how slow of understanding are they all in all spiritual things, their ignorance splitting them into many sects—the man as dull as the little child—like as the Israelites of old were blind to the goodness of the Messiah, so are the dull conceited nations blind to the holiness and wisdom of the Holy Scriptures, exhibiting their dulness by almost ignoring their existence.

Listen, and I will tell thee how the minds of men have become perverted and filled with superstitious nonsense; some with adulterated Scriptures, some robbed altogether of their birthright, the Holy Word of God, by evil men.

The love of notoriety has led evil men in all ages to teach ignorant men sophistical doctrines, which those ignorant men blindly followed; even the Holy Scriptures were perverted, and false notions of the Messiah were disseminated, so that the Israelites of old knew not the Holy Messiah when they saw him and heard his words, neither would they believe him when he said he was truly the Messiah. In like manner, the love of notoriety led unworthy Gentile converts, even during the lifetime of the Apostles, to pervert the Gospel by strange teachings and by idolatrous practices, thereby leading astray many others of the Gentile converts who had before given up their idolatrous practices, so that those unworthy Gentile teachers and their followers were rebuked by the Apostles; nevertheless they continued. During the first three centuries after the death of Christ, His followers were persecuted sorely, so that the most pious and freest from idolatry were slain by savage men—murderers as were the murderers of the holy Messiah; fastening their guilt upon their brethren, all the children of Adam. Printing being then unknown, and for more than a thousand years thereafter, the written Scriptures were scarce, and very few were able to read; therefore ignorance was almost universal, so that what men knew of them was almost wholly from hearsay; thus error after error was disseminated, and became so incorporated with the true doctrines of Christ that even well-meaning pious men, through the errors instilled into them during childhood, could not distinguish the true from the false. Foolish notions among these people were plentiful, and controversy violent. While in this state of spiritual ignorance and disorder, the Emperor Charlemagne made the Bishop of Rome Pope, head of all who called themselves Christians, that the Pope might overrule all disputants in spiritual things, and compel them to become quiet. Worldly ambition seized the Popes successively, who imagined that, by working upon the superstitious fears of men, they might, in time, bend the whole world to their will. Little by little, armies of spurious priests, wearing the mask of goodness, were organised and sent into many countries, having, as it were, a commmander-in-chief (the Pope), generals (cardinals), colonels (archbishops), majors (bishops), captains, lieutenants, ensigns, over the rank and file of priests; these conquered and subdued the ignorant people of those countries by their greater educated subtlety, and by craftily siding with nation warring against nation—wholly against the precepts of Christ the Messiah. This compact army of priests, satisfied with the position and reverence accorded them, united themselves strongly in the bonds of discipline and subordination towards their chief, the Pope, and became in the sight of men very strong. This army of spurious priests worked as one man, and by subtlety compelled the exhausted emperors and kings to humble themselves to the Pope, as their master, forbidding all to read the Scriptures, destroying all beneath their sway who did so, branding themselves a murdering sect—murderers of the children of God—impiously usurping the judgeship of the Messiah, while really possessing the foolishness and cruelty of cruel wolves. The Popes thus became paramount over a considerable portion of the Earth, and in their pride claimed as theirs the sole right to appoint kings as their servants, compelling some of the most abject emperors and kings to hold the stirrup of the Pope's mule, while he mounted and dismounted, as a sign to all men that the Pope was the greatest among men, nay, something more than man.

The false doctrines of the early Christians the Popes perpetuated, and invented other false doctrines ; the Papacy mystified the people and themselves with a mixture of Christianity and idolatry, thereby craftily founding in the sight of men the most powerful empire men have seen, having absolute sway over many nations, but which the light of God's Holy Word will fast crumble into pieces, soon to be no more seen upon the earth for ever.

The Papacy, that army of victorious, crafty, spurious priests, not satisfied with the power exercised over the kings of the earth, demanded and enforced under pain of death, implicit obedience in all things and abasing reverence to every priest, and impudently and impiously instilled into the minds of their frightened followers, whose minds they had purposely filled with superstitious nonsense during childhood, that with them rested the supernatural power of giving their souls entrance into heaven, or sending them into hell, and called their chief "His Holiness" and "Holy Father" as though he were God, who is really the only Holy Father.

These spurious crafty priests were guardians—not of the Scriptures, for the reading of these they forbade—but were the guards of the Papacy and disseminators of tradition concocted to uphold the Papacy; they were guards who did not murder with their own hands, but secretly incited the civil and military powers of the several nations to murder and smite with theirs. They have been, and still are, the most subtle and impious of men, and by their numbers, the compactness of their priestly army, and their concentrated machinations against any one nation, are powerful enemies to the disunited other sects, and to the foolish nations who give them footing—impostors, seeking to perpetuate their authority through frightening the timid and superstitious, by falsely claiming supernatural power over them.

The Papacy desires to sow dissension in the midst of an opposing nation, to concentrate the craft and subtlety of the spurious priests dispersed among the nations upon it, and get the mastery; even to stir up the nations bending beneath her sway to dip their hands in the blood of the nations, herself the murderess. Foolish nations! why dally ye with one so red? know you not that he who consorts with the vile becomes himself also vile—one who uses the name of your Lord for the sake only of her vile ambition? Look around you upon the nations who own her sway, how pitiable, how miserable are they, because they are blind, because they have been filled with superstition and have become foolish and idolatrous, and because of their utter ignorance of the Holy Word of God. Well may the spread of the Holy Scriptures be to her a great terror; for in their spread she sees her downfall, and through their spread the numerous Papal army will become as powerless as a rope of sand and quickly disappear for ever. The voice of God will silence them.

Nations will hereafter read with pity and holy anger that every city under the Papal sway has its patron saint; nay, every handicraft also; nay every man, also, his patron saint, like the pagans of old, and so far imitating them as to set-up and worship an imaginary Queen of Heaven; 'and that to these supposed beings men bow the knee and pray, foolishly thinking they can see and hear everything throughout the world, as though they were gods, possessing power to be their guardians and to shield them from all earthly harm—as thought similarly the Romans, Greeks, and other pagans of old —the Pope, their saint-maker, canonising whom he pleases, and desiring the people to adore, like Nebuchadnezzar, whomsoever he may set up, worshipping them as gods, but thinking to cheat God by calling them the lesser name— saints—the Popes impiously claiming to be infallible as God Himself.

Through these great Papal evils mankind have been cheated out of their birthright—the Holy Scriptures—by lying, ambitious, spurious priests; and so wickedness has been doubly victorious throughout the world for about 1800 years; during that time the Messiah seems almost to have died in vain; as men were after the fall of Adam to the deluge, so have they been after the mediatory death of the Messiah until now, few understanding the Holy Scriptures aright, few worshipping God without images.

Ye foolish nations, smitten by the Papacy with superstition and with folly, why suffer ye the Papal brand of discord to rend you asunder and sow hatred among your people? You permit no other foreign king to exercise sway in the midst of your nation, to breed rebellion and sow dissension for his own crafty ends among you; neither permit the Papal king nor his spurious priests, the crafty pretenders to supernatural power. Verily the Papacy, that fomentor of discord and impiety, is a cunning device of cunning men to obtain and hold dominion over the nations—of men using the cloak of priesthood to hide their love of ease, their love of reverence, and their love of power. Foolish nations! to be thus deceived and thus to submit to the yoke like the horse or the ox; verily strife and bloodshed, dissension, and mutual hate have whipped you for your folly, and will whip you until you become less foolish; your children's children will be wiser than yourselves.

CHAPTER X.

IT is easier for a foolish generation to continue foolish than to become sensible, because, oh ye nations, your governors are too selfish, too conceited, too luxurious, too dishonest, too grasping, too unchaste, too frivolous, too superstitious, and too irreligious; for as your governors are, so imitate the people, winking at each other's follies. Ye do not, oh ye nations, sufficiently abhor the spiritual deceivers of your people, nor your grasping, nor your selfish, nor your luxurious, nor your conceited, nor your dishonest, nor your unchaste, nor your frivolous, nor your superstitious, nor sufficiently have the love of God nor love for your fellow men in your hearts; neither do you sufficiently abhor your liars, nor your violent; therefore your people are harassed and oppressed, oppressing and harassing each other. Ye will deem it, ye thoughtless people of this generation, less troublesome to continue in your foolish ways, to continue unrestrained, than to change your thoughts, to be, as it were, a little child commencing to learn afresh; therefore ye will continue to be foolish. But suffer your little ones, oh ye nations, to be taught aright, that they may be less miserable than yourselves; in this thing be sensible, in this thing resolutely and perseveringly do your duty.

Behold the time is at hand, even knocking at the door, when the judgment of men will become clear, and they will be able, by their common sense, to distinguish pure worship from that which is spurious, and those human lions, the men of strength and violence, will become as those human lambs, the peaceful men, and spiritual wisdom and kindness will reign in the hearts of all men; but not yet, for troublous times are upon you, oh ye nations of the whole world, because of the forgetfulness of your forefathers, and of your own forgetfulness of God. Like as a leafy tree is shaken by the blast, so will your minds be shaken violently. The spiritual nonsense that has been instilled into your souls will be shattered to pieces, like as an earthen vessel hurled against a rock; ye will not be destroyed, but ye will come out of your troubles as wise men, for ye will then understand that it is better to obey the advice of God than to put your trust in the advice of men who know not God; or of those who advise you to obey God spuriously, obeying him, like as do the Papacy, a little, but disobeying him greatly; and the ministers of the many other spurious sects will strive, from unworthy motives, to perpetuate the separation of their own sects from every other sect, and will beguile the silly sheep of their flocks; but the others will not suffer themselves to be beguiled, but will cast off those unworthy teachers contemptuously, for it is not the sheep who wilfully go wrong but the unworthy shepherds, who, for their own selfishness and ease, will strive to keep them in the evil paths they have been accustomed to. Your own wickedness, oh ye nations, will chastise you, for the wicked will chastise the wicked—your God looking on with pity, but permitting you to be chastised—for through chastisement alone will you harken to his words; through chastisement alone will you sweep away from among you your spurious Churches, and your many spurious sects, and bind yourselves together, as loving brethren, into one Universal Church, the Church of the Messiah, Christ your king; then will you know what it is to have the Holy Spirit of Christ among you, having Christ, not bodily upon earth, but like as the Holy Spirit of God is present in the Holy Scriptures.

Troublous times are upon you, oh ye nations of the whole world, because the men of violence and the men of ignorance will be stirred up by the spurious priests of the many spurious sects to imbrue their hands in the blood of their fellow men, to oppress and persecute them that the spurious priests may still hold sway, and there will be great divisions through your ignorance of the Holy Scriptures; but the spiritually wise will quickly prevail and the ignorant become spiritually wise. The spurious ministers, the sowers of superstition, of nonsense, and of hatred among men, will not be converted, but all power to do further evil will be taken from them by their fellow-men. By the free-will of man, man became disobedient towards God, and thereby filled the earth with unholiness, violence, and misery; and by the free-will of man, man will become obedient towards God. The nations will acknowledge the Messiah to be their king—not through any miracle, but from conviction of the soul—the Jewish nation first, preparatory to their repossessing the land of their forefathers. Then will the nations of the whole earth become a holy people in the sight of God, and happiness be their portion for ever, and their teachers and rulers will be spiritually wise and the people will no more fall into error, but become as wise in spiritual things as their teachers, and the Holy Messiah, the king of that portion of the heavens set aside by God for the everlasting home of the souls of pardoned men, will be their acknowledged king, and he will reign in their hearts, and His precepts in the Holy Scriptures sway their thoughts, and he in heaven, before his God and Father, will acknowledge them to be his ransomed children.

Be ye watchful, therefore, oh ye true Christians in every land, rise up and quickly band yourselves together, for troublous times are upon you. Haste! spread this little book among the nations. God will assist men, but only through their obedience to His advice, as recorded in the Holy Scriptures, will He assist them.

CHAPTER XI.

Unity among Mankind.

THE many spiritual sects have false and foolish notions of God; therefore they differ one from the other, and look upon each other as enemies, despising one another. By their disunion and hatred they are powerless in stemming the evil tendencies of the evil-disposed, and so wickedness everywhere is rampant; they cause men to become evil and continue evil-disposed, for the evil-disposed have the wit to see that their diverse notions must necessarily be erroneous, so that like as the many sects despise each other, so do the evil-disposed despise the many sects. Men are discordant one with the other in spiritual matters, and therefore in temporal things, because they err, not rightly understanding the Holy Scriptures; the many sects each see the mote in every other sect, and therefore keep apart from them. Men err because they are wrongly taught; some are altogether ignorant of the Word of God, others, through their erring teachers, misunderstand the spirit of the Holy Scriptures, dwelling much on certain parts, almost ignoring other portions, and so fall into error—one sect preferring one part, another sect preferring other parts, and so their thoughts become discordant; it is as a whole the Holy Scriptures must be taken.

The teachings of the Holy Scriptures are —
1. There is but *one* God.

2. That God prompted holy men to write the Scriptures; therefore they are the true Word of God.

3. That Jesus Christ was veritably the long promised Messiah of God.

4. The Messiah is not God, but an angel chosen before the creation of the starry skies by God to be the Messiah.

5. That the Messiah is now the king of that portion of the heavens set aside by God as the everlasting home of the souls of pardoned men, and that all true worshippers of God through the mediatory death of Christ will enter the Messiah's kingdom in heaven after their decease and live with him there for ever.

6. God is a lover of all that is good, all that is holy, and desires us to be loving, tender-hearted, and just one to the other. God is a hater of evil, and desires us to hate all evil things and refrain from all those things that are evil.

These six things constitute the whole spirit of the Holy Scriptures—they form the one theme of every holy writer, and of the Messiah, Christ himself. Now, ye zealous worshippers of God, call assemblages of the people, and enquire of them if these things are not the one theme of the Holy Word of God, and they will quickly give their assent, and many will unite themselves into one holy bond of brotherhood, and form one Universal Church, the old Church of Christ—a Church which has been in abeyance since the days of the Apostles of the Messiah, Christ. Then will the Church of Christ come out, like himself, the victor over the evils of the world, and the Holy Spirit of God will lead them safely through the troublous times that now enwrap the earth.

PART III.

WHAT THE SCRIPTURES TEACH.

CHAPTER I.

THE ATTRIBUTES OF GOD.

GOD is everywhere, and surrounds all things, like as the waters of the sea surround the fishes in the sea; God has a knowledge of everything that takes place—the most secret as well as the most open; He is the source of all wisdom and power—these are the attributes of God. There is only one God, who is *one* holy Being. God is indestructible; therefore He lives for ever: all else may change, but the one holy God—the source of all good things—does not change; He is the same from illimitable time past to illimitable time to come.

Worship is speaking reverently to the unseen God—believing Him to be near by listening and observing—speaking as confidingly to the unseen God as a man blind from his birth talks to his listening mother, whom he has never seen, and of whose shape and colour he has no knowledge.

God is a living spirit, and not flesh and blood—a spirit, in that no man has seen him. Nevertheless, we know He exists because of the mighty, wondrous things that everywhere surround us—the sun, the moon, the stars, and this round earth and all the marvels our eyes behold—and we also know that the Holy Scriptures are the revelation of God to man; therefore, although we cannot see the living God, we know He is everywhere surrounding us, seeing us, and hearing us. God is a spirit, as invisible to the eyes of man as is the self-will; yet as truly near—nay, nearer—to every living creature than clouds are near to a blind man, but which he neither sees, nor feels, nor smells, nor hears—it is the will of God that neither the blind man should see the clouds, nor any living earthly creature see Him.

The Glory of God, His condensed self,—which is His glorious person, visible to the angels as a holy, living being—is in the immeasurable heavens which surround the starry skies where He has His dwelling place, surrounded by innumerable happy angel spirits, and His glorious Son, our Redeemer and Heavenly King, Jesus Christ. All outside His glorious person is His Holy Spirit—a part of himself, an invisible cloud (like as the body of a bird and its wings form *one* bird) filling all space—so that God is everywhere, and there is of course not room for any other God, neither is there really any other God. The King Christ and all the other angels of God, and all the saints in heaven, and all the stars, and everything everywhere, live, and move, and are in the midst of the Holy, living Spirit of God, like as the fishes of the sea move in the midst of the waters of the sea.

There is no sun nor moon in heaven, for God Himself is the light thereof—He is the living sun of heaven, seen only by angel spirits, the saints in heaven, and His glorious Messiah.

CHAPTER II.

Before Creation.

GOD, who has ever existed as He now exists and will exist for ever, and in whose sight a thousand years are less than a moment to man, determined to found a kingdom in heaven for the angel Christ, a holy angel then living amid innumerable other angels with God, who should be the King thereof. It was necessary the future King should have subjects, and it was absolutely necessary that His subjects should be perfectly holy in the sight of God, for in no part of heaven is there unholiness—holiness consists in obeying the laws of God—perfectly obedient to their King, Christ, and yet have perfect freedom, not being coerced in any way (for it is only the rebelliously inclined who require to be coerced), perfectly obedient because having perfect knowledge instilled into them that perfect obedience to their Holy King induced perfect happiness to all, therefore delighting in being holy. All things are possible with God, so that He might have peopled the kingdom of Christ in heaven in many ways: therefore God purposed to create a body of flesh and blood—giving it life by giving it motion—and unite it to a part of His living breath, which God called the soul, that the twain,

1. The living flesh and blood,
2. The living soul,

should form one male man, out of whom should proceed countless millions of children, each possessing a portion of the one soul.

The law of Justice as laid down in the Holy Scriptures by the Lord God, is the forfeiture of an eye for the spiteful removal of an eye—a tooth for the spiteful removal of a tooth—the forfeiture of a life for the spiteful taking away of the life of man—the forfeiture of everlasting life should the intended new being—man—disobey God, and the forfeiture of a perfectly holy life to redeem from everlasting death the intended new being—man—should he become disobedient and thereby unholy, and need in consequence a redeemer.

And God purposed that out of the male man should

proceed a female man, that from them might proceed countless millions of their kind; the countless millions possessing between them the one life of the body united to the one life of the soul, which should constitute the male man, so that the countless millions might also be really and truly man, in like manner as a lump of gold may be divided into countless millions of atoms, each atom being as purely gold as the great lump. These intended new beings would necessarily have to be endowed with passions for perpetuating their kind, which passions were unknown in heaven, therefore, the new beings would thus far be inferior to the angels of heaven. God, therefore, determined to build a habitation outside of heaven, which should be glorious within and gloriously set in the midst of innumerable stars. He deemed it necessary that the future subjects of the Heavenly King, Jesus Christ, should, before they became His subjects in heaven, live and multiply in their new earthly home, as it were in school, for a time, and then be carried lovingly into heaven into Christ's kingdom, there to live for ever with Him.

CHAPTER III.
The Creation.

BEFORE the sun, the moon, the countless stars, and this round earth were created, all that vast space within reach of the telescopes of man during a clear and starry night, and immeasurably far, far beyond, was filled with gaseous matter without life, shape, or motion. Four different kinds only of inert gaseous matter were there,

1. Oxygen,
2. Hydrogen,
3. Nitrogen,
4. Latent heat.

Diffused throughout this cloudy matter was the Holy Spirit of God, which, extending everywhere beyond the glorious Person of God in heaven, was here also; all was dark, all was silent, all was dead—as it were space in fallow, awaiting to be fashioned anew—the Holy Spirit of God that was in its midst, was alone imbued with life. At length God purposed to make man, and create for him a round world as a temporary habitation, beautiful within, and beautiful outside of it, like a bride bedecked with jewels.

The Holy Spirit of God moved amid the inert gaseous matter, giving it motion; and God said, "Let there be light," and instantly all the latent heat throughout that heretofore dark, quiet, vast space rushed to one spot, and in twenty-four hours all had accumulated together and formed the sun—the sun being dark, not yet shedding any light. This occupied the first day.

On the second day, God gave the word, and instantly the sun burst forth a glorious mass of light, and the electrical flames darted throughout that second day into the midst of the cloud of hydrogen, oxygen and nitrogen, vivifying them thereby, causing violent chemical action, which produced a strong mutual attraction between the interspersed atoms, which had the effect of causing all the then vivified matter to condense into great solid balls in millions—occupying the second day. The space between each ball was left perfectly vacuous of everything excepting the electrical heat that is constantly being poured into them from the electric sun. These new-made balls attracted a continuous stream of electric flame from the sun, so condensed and so vast in that one day as would take tens of thousands of years now to equal—pulverising the surface of one of them, the earth.

On the third day, God prepared one of the solid balls for the habitation of man. The softened mountains were raised above the lower land, seas were formed, vegetation was created and made rapidly to grow in the electrified virgin soil.

On the fourth day, God placed one of the balls—the moon—near to the earth, that it might by night reflect upon the round earth the light of the sun, and with the sun induce tides, produce winds, and generate moisture. God also devised the motion of the moon round the earth, and the revolution of the earth round the sun, and the revolution of the earth on its own axis once every twenty-four hours. He also made the earth to oscillate, each pole turning alternately inwardly towards the sun very slowly, at the rate of one complete oscillation every year—thereby producing day and night and the seasons, letting them be for signs and seasons, for days and years; and gave motion to the planets, to give variety to the starry skies, in like manner as He has given variety to vegetation and to all things.

On the fifth day, God said, "Let the waters bring forth abundantly the moving creature that hath life, and fowl that may fly above in the air; and God created great whales, and every living creature that moveth, which the waters afterwards brought forth abundantly after their kind, and every winged fowl after his kind; and God saw it was good. And the evening and the morning (day and night) were the fifth day."

On the sixth day, God said, "Let the earth bring forth the living creature after his kind, and creeping thing and beast of the field after his kind; and it was so, and God saw it was very good. And God said, Let us make man in our image, after our likeness, and let them have dominion over the fishes of the sea, and over every living creature. So God created man in His own image, male and female created He them"—Adam being the only created living man, but having stored within him the germs of innumerable male and female men; Eve being the first-born woman.

God stored in the males of every species of living things many varieties of the same species, varying them in their shape, colour, strength and size, some varieties being more numerous than others; so that, in like manner as no two trees are exactly alike, even of the same species, so no two living creatures nor vegetation, even of the same species, should be exactly alike. Some varieties have now run their course, becoming extinct; others are just commencing to be born. Thus has God given variety to all living things, in all ages; only those which He created during the six days can possibly be born. Moreover, God has so contrived that all living things of the same species should differ in many things inwardly and outwardly, their mode of life influencing their appearance; so that, in like manner as an evil man bears upon his countenance a stamp differing from the days of his innocent childhood, so God detects the degree of evil in every living thing by its difference from its first parents, when fresh out of his hands during the six days of creation.

God gave to every living creature self-will, first to desire and then to do—some things to do intuitively, without thought, neither knowing nor seeing the internal mechanism of their body—and has furnished them with brain-nerves, that photographic impressions thereon of what they see, hear, smell, taste, and feel may enable them to remember; but to living vegetation God gave neither eyes, nor ears, nor taste, nor smell, nor brain, nor inherent power to roam, but gave it inherent power to perpetuate its kind, to obtain food, and to grow.

Thus was made in six days the vast electrical sun, the great sustainer of earthly life, without which nothing would be solid, but gaseous, as before creation, yet but an inanimate ball, as inanimate as a lighted candle, the mainspring, as it were, of the firmament. Also were made the moon, the countless stars, and this round earth, with all its wondrous contents. The intense electrical light of the sun illumines the countless stars, and moon, and earth, causing them to shine, which, but for its brilliant light, would be as dark balls in a dark place—unseen. On the seventh day God ended His work which He had made, and He rested on the seventh day, and blessed it, and afterwards ordained that all men, and all their beasts of burden, should rest from servile work on that day—on every seventh day—and be perfectly free—the poor man as free as the rich, the beast as well as the man—it being necessary, lest the thoughts of men should be engrossed by the things of earth.

There is a limit to the starry skies, but the heavens which surround them are illimitable.

CHAPTER IV.

The Creation of Adam.

THE Scriptures teach that Adam was the only *one* of all mankind whom God created without being born.

In like manner as the Lord God had made every other living creature out of the dust of the earth, so He formed the flesh and blood of Adam, which, being of the earth, and visible to earthly eyes, and made *male*, was not like God. The Lord God then gave to Adam that holy thing, the soul, by breathing into his nostrils, and Adam thereby became a living man. The two lives—

1. The life of the flesh and blood,
2. The life of the soul,

constituted the man Adam. The *only* life of the body, and the only soul that God has given to Adam and his descendants—the breath of God, a part of His invisible Holy Spirit, constituting the invisible soul of Adam, the only part of Adam that was like God. Behold, oh man! in the brute gorilla an image of thyself as thyself would be if thou hadst not a soul—that jewel from heaven, in which only thou art like God.

Mark well, for this is the *key of wisdom*. God has given only *one* living body and only *one* living soul to Adam, the twain constituting one person, man. From this twain the living body of all mankind, and the living soul of every man, are derived, thereby constituting them the offspring of Adam. God stored in Adam the seed of the body and the seed of the soul in temporary union, hiding some of the united seed deeply within many folds, others in but few, that some might be born within a few years, and some not till after the lapse of many ages. These seeds had the germ of mankind within them. All inherit, through their fathers' right up to Adam, the shape of Adam, but only some see the light of day, and are born into the world as separate beings; some of the born become worthless in the sight of God through their folly, but others produce the fruit of holiness unto the Lord. These constitute His living, holy harvest, for they are His holy children. Man perpetuates his kind, and all other living creatures and all vegetation their kind, according as God created their seed.

God has not created anything after the sixth day. Every living creature and all vegetation have proceeded from the few which God made during the six days of creation. They existed in an undeveloped state in those ancient ones; but were not *born* into the world as separate beings—living things *proceeding* through the male line only, being *developed* through the female line only. Thus, male and female are equally necessary, excepting in the case of Adam and in the case of the Virgin Mary.

God also, on the sixth day, made the germ of *another* living body similar to the body of Adam. This living germ God reserved for some future day, wherewith to constitute the flesh and blood of Christ, and which God long afterwards placed in the womb of the pure Virgin Mary, to be there *developed* and born as the child Jesus Christ, the living spirit of Christ being carried by God from Heaven, and united thereto at the instant of birth.

Adam was created a little lower than the angels of Heaven, inasmuch as his heavenly soul was tied, as it were, to his earthly body—a body like that of the then innocent brutes, that he might have numerous descendants. He was an angel of earth, pure and spotless, and all the living seed within him of the unborn countless millions of mankind were also holy, pure, and spotless.

CHAPTER V.

The Birth of Eve.

ADAM was the last of all things which God created. In him God created and placed the germs of all his descendants—of all mankind—male and female. God designed that the *one* earthly lord, Adam, should, like all other creatures, have a helpmate worthy of him; and, causing Adam to fall into a deep sleep, God caused the beauteous female infant Eve to issue from a rib of Adam. The infant Eve was thus born out of the man Adam. Thus was Eve the first of all *born* creatures; and thus did Eve have no mother, in like manner as in long years afterwards the Holy Messiah had no earthly father.

Out of Adam was *born* the infant Eve, that Adam might be the *one* earthly lord and the *one* earthly father of all mankind. The man Adam and the female Eve were perfectly holy and in constant communion with God, keeping the desires of their bodies wholly subject to their souls; they were as brother and sister, perfectly happy and perfectly innocent, as are the angels of heaven, for they had God always with them during many years, communing with them and teaching them; they were not yet free to act, for what Adam said and did, and Eve also, were done by God prompting them, thereby teaching them what was good; they were, therefore, wiser than all their descendants in all things which conduced to their happiness; and all other living creatures were perfectly happy, the lion and the lamb resting together in perfect peace, eating herbage; there was no fear in all the world, for the presence of the Holy Person of God shed upon them and upon all living creatures a feeling of perfect purity, of perfect peace, and perfect contentment. The Holy Person of God could then come into the world, because everything in it was good.

The Lord God did not create Adam a perfect being—not so perfect as are the angels of heaven—inasmuch as prayer. praise, and thanksgiving to God were not yet forthcoming from Adam of his own free-will; his soul was not yet free to act, for what Adam and Eve did and said were done by God prompting them, and so teaching them what was the principle of goodness; at length God left them to act of their own free-will without prompting. The Lord God having taught them all that was requisite for them to know, was desirous of testing the obedience of these earthly angels, the chief work of His creating, and warning them to keep their bodies, their earthly part, in entire subjection to their souls, their heavenly part—declaring that disobedience to these His commands should entail His anger—God thereupon left them for the first time in their lives to act of their own free-will without His prompting, and God then withdrew His Holy Person from the earth, but His Holy Spirit, the living invisible cloud, still remained.

CHAPTER VI.

The Sin of Disobedience brought into the World.

THE withdrawal of the Holy Person of God everywhere wrought a great change, for it was His Holy Personal Presence which maintained all things in a state of perfect purity and holiness; for, some time afterwards, the woman Eve saw the serpent doing that which the Lord God commanded Adam and Eve not to do, the serpent not having been forbidden because it was a beast of the field, its obedience to God not being put to the proof. Thereupon a strong inclination of the body came upon Eve, and she reasoned within herself, thereby increasing her inclination to do what God had commanded her not to do. Now, the reasoning faculty of the flesh and blood of man, which is the mind, also called self-will, and which Adam possessed before God breathed into his nostrils, and which *all* living creatures possess, the cat and the dog, and all else—was more subtle in reasoning than that of every other living creature; the mind being, as it were, the silent advocate of the flesh and blood, argues for the gratification of the longings of the body—whereas the soul, being of heaven, silently argues in favour of the wisdom of perfect obedience of the whole person, of body and soul, to the will of God, in that the will of the body and the will of the soul should jointly be wholly guided by the precepts of God. There is therefore a perpetual silent antagonism between these two powers, the brutish one tending to evil, and the angelic one to good, in every one of mankind.

The will of the body, its brutish passions, is sometimes called in Scripture the *evil power*, because it was the carnal passions of the body of Adam which was overcome by the great temptation, and which continues to be the great tempter to do evil —sometimes it is called *sin*, sometimes the *devil*, sometimes *satan*, sometimes the *serpent*, because it was a serpent which unwittingly roused the passions of Eve, and the right knowledge of the soul is sometimes called *conscience*. The brutish body, longing for what its eyes can see, and for the gratification of its passions unrestrainedly, and satisfied with the things of earth; the other, the immortal heavenly soul, longing to return to its native home in heaven where the Holy Person of God is—deriving no satisfaction in things of the earth, because of the evils therein.

The brutish body of Eve, therefore, owing to the subtle reasoning of her mind, felt a very great longing, and—tempting Adam—they disobeyed God, the first of all living creatures that dared to disobey Him. Thus did Adam fall under the one great test, and thus was wickedness brought into the world, and God satisfied Himself that the brutish body of man was unworthy to enter heaven. The man and the woman then became aware what it was to be good and what it was to be evil in the sight of God—their conscience smote them, and they were ashamed and afraid of the promised coming of God, their Creator.

CHAPTER VII.

The Soul of Adam is Cursed and the brutish Body (the chief offender) Condemned to Everlasting Death.

THE holy anger of the Lord God was very great against them for their disobedience, and He took away from their brutish body perpetual life, so that after a time it should *die* for ever, and ignominiously become corrupt, and become again, so long as the round earth existed, as part of the ground whence it was first taken; and God condemned the unenergetic soul to sleep after its separation from the dead body, until the offspring of a pure virgin (the Messiah) should, by His perfect holiness as man, regain the victory of the body of man over the passions of the body, and so restore mankind to the favour of God, who then would remove the curse wherewith God cursed the soul of Adam—so that, through the merits of the Messiah, God his Father and our Father might be with us once more as before the fall, not indeed in Person, but in His love; and might, in justice to His own Holiness, be able to pardon those of mankind who may have the wisdom to trust in the promises of God, worshipping Him.

Thus did those angels of earth, Adam and Eve, fall under the displeasure of God, and all the living seed within Adam became unholy and impure in the sight of the Almighty Creator, for the seed was part of Adam. And God gave Eve to be Adam's wife, and unto them was born their eldest child, Cain, conceived in sin, pre-eminently inheriting the great transgression. Nevertheless, God in His mercy blessed Adam and Eve, and said unto them, "Be fruitful and multiply, and replenish the earth and subdue it, and have dominion over the fish of the sea, and over the fowl of the air, and over every living creature that moveth upon the earth. And God said, Behold, I have given you every herb which is upon the face of the earth, and every tree in which is the fruit of a tree yielding fruit, to you it shall be given."

The great disobedience of Adam and Eve having made this round earth unholy in the sight of God, He withdrew His holy Person from the earth altogether. From this first disobedient act is derived all the pain, all the sorrow, all the wickedness, that has since afflicted the world—the man Adam, and the woman Eve, lost the gentle nobility of their deportment, and their sweetness of expression, and their descendants became still more stamped with the brutish passions, as their descendants became more vile, deteriorating in like manner as the brutes have deteriorated in their appearance—from the gentleness of their first parents before the fall. Through the great transgression this once beautiful earth, everywhere a paradise, where innocence and peace reigned, has been transformed into what it is—the ground lost its great fertility, the air and the waters their perfect purity—the living creatures of the land, of the air, of the water, and vegetation, their harmlessness, and acquired injurious properties (like as an innocent child oft becomes a vile man), increasing with the wickedness of man; the garden rose degenerated into the wild rose, and in like manner did man and all things degenerate. The round earth was no longer everywhere a garden, no longer were the lesser living things harmless one to the other, for envy and strife rose in their midst. the strong chased the less strong, some thereby became courageous and some fearful; the several members of their bodies became altered, their natures gradually changed, and the courageous, the fearful, and the other strong impressions of the parents were transmitted to their offspring, and became to them as instinct. Vegetation became impure and poisonous. The air and the water became corrupt, breeding famine and pestilence, and the flesh of the cruel creatures of the land, of the air, and of the water, became unfit as food for man; and God long afterwards forbad His people, the Israelites, to eat them, for they became poisonous and injurious, but to eat only such of the land creatures as feed on grass. The happiness of the earth was wrecked.

Adam's transgression has been succeeded by *our* many transgressions, therefore the Holy Person of God continues to keep far away from the earth, but His Holy Spirit, part of Himself (as the wings of a bird are part of the bird), He has not withdrawn, that He might save those who comprehend and worship Him.

CHAPTER VIII.

The Deluge.

THE children of Adam multiplied greatly, for women greatly exceeded in number the men; the life of the body was strong within them and they became sensual. They allowed their passions free scope, and because they could not see God they forgot Him. Cruelty and every species of wickedness were prevalent, and it grieved the Lord God that He had made man, for man had become very offensive in His sight, and God said, " I will destroy man whom I have created ; both man and beast, and creeping thing, and the fowls of the air, for it grieveth me that I have made them." And God looked upon the round Earth, and behold it was very impure, and God listened in vain for the penitent cry and worship of man, for every living thing had departed from the purity and innocence which God gave them at the beginning. Cruelty and wickedness reigned everywhere, and mankind was as the beast of the field, steeped in foolishness, and utterly forgetful of God, as though they had no souls in them. Noah only found favour in the sight of God, for he was a just and God-fearing man; and God commanded Noah to build an Ark, and take into it a few favourable specimens of every species of creeping thing, and of every living creature to keep seed alive—of every species, not of every colour or variety of species, for of living creatures there are countless varieties, all proceeding from the few species which God made on the fifth and sixth days of creation, so that some varieties that had existence before the Deluge became extinct, through the Deluge. And Noah took into the Ark the most favourable specimens of each of the few species. Behold! oh man! how greatly thy kind varies in colour, in size, in deportment, in shape. Compare the most holy with the most brutal, and note the vast difference in the twain. Nevertheless all men proceed from the man Adam.

Every one of the living creatures saved in the Ark had less strength of life than their first ancestors, and therefore subsequently lived a less number of years and grew to less stature, a portion of vitality having been retained by their several ancestors. The *one* life of the body being transmitted by the male—the female simply developing—every life therefore transmitted by the male lessens his vitality and his progeny possesses less than he himself first had.

And God commanded Noah to take into the Ark a few of every species again to re-people the earth, of fowls of the air, of cattle, and of every creeping thing, together with the family of Noah. And God caused a violent Deluge, with storms of wind, to sweep over the whole round Earth, and every living creature excepting those in the Ark were destroyed; the waters of the ocean rolled over the highest mountains, sweeping into destruction every living creature that had taken refuge there. After the lapse of about three hundred days, the waters became confined to their present boundaries, forming the seas and great rivers as we now see them. Noah, his family, and all the living creatures then came out of the Ark, and God promised the terrified Noah that He would not again deluge the whole world with water.

Thus, after an interval of about sixteen hundred years from the creation of the starry skies, did the great Deluge alter the whole surface of the Earth. The Deluge came upon the Earth wholly through the wickedness of man. God had satisfied Himself that none but the family of Noah, through the holiness of Noah, was worthy to live even upon the Earth. And God stored up for future men, in the depths of the Earth, rich fuel, by causing the trees that were torn up by the Deluge, to accumulate in masses and sink to the bottom of the muddy waters, with the natural sap in them, that it might help to convert the fibrous wood into coal, and to sink horizontally in layers at intervals of time during the Deluge, piling it only in what God intended should be habitable land, that it might not be wasted.

CHAPTER IX.

After the Deluge.

MANKIND quickly multiplied upon the Earth, for the daughters of men were in those early ages of the world more numerous than the sons, so that every man had several wives, and Noah was the earthly lord over all the children of men; to him they made obesiance as to one from whose loins all had proceeded, and his sons were men of authority and reverence among them.

The long life attained by the descendants of Adam before the Deluge enabled them to attain great *worldly* knowledge ; some of this knowledge was known to Noah, his sons, his daughters, and his daughters-in-law, which they in their turn communicated to their descendants after the Deluge, and so gave the new era a strong starting point in things appertaining to worldly knowledge ; and God put it into the hearts of men to disperse themselves with their wives and children over the face of the Earth. And the bold collected round them the families of their friends and founded separate tribes ; and the bold with their families, were continually spreading themselves over the Earth, and many became men of renown and men of violence.

The speech of men, which mankind had learnt one from the other, and from their father Noah, became varied, so that the separated tribes spoke differently, and tribes distant one from the other could not understand the speech one of the other. And the tribes kept themselves apart through jealousy, fear and distrust one of the other, and their notions of God became hazy. As mankind increased in ignorance of God, so did their thoughts concerning Him differ : superstition and error took the place of common sense, and mankind down to these days have perpetuated the senselessness of their forefathers. And many forgot much of the worldly knowledge taught the children of men by Noah and his family, and in spiritual things and in worldly things also they became men of ignorance. Thus did the many tribes overspread the earth, and thus did they trace their pedigree from the bold ones, their chiefs, sometimes right up to Noah—the more prosperous settled tribes ruled over by the sons of Noah, and their eldest sons commenced their history from the holy man Noah, their father and their lord.

After the lapse of about two hundred and ninety years from the time of the deluge, Abraham was born, Noah being still alive. Abraham became a just and holy man and greatly pleased God, inasmuch as he was very teachable and worshipped God without images. For Abraham was surrounded by men who had ignorantly formed hazy notions of God, and therefore used images in their worship. What the forbidden fruit was to Adam and Eve, images have been to the ignorant, the superstitious, and the weak of faith, in all ages—their great temptation. God made Himself known to Abraham, and communed with him, and God tested the faith of Abraham and found it sound. The faith and obedience of Abraham greatly pleased God, who promised, before and at the time of his death, that his descendants should become very numerous and be the favoured people of God. And God told Abraham that within him was the germ of the woman who as a pure virgin should give birth to the Messiah, the deliverer of the souls of men. This promise and revelation were repeated to Isaac, the only son of Abraham, to Jacob, the son of Isaac, and long afterwards again to David, a descendant of Jacob; these greatly rejoicing because of the promised Messiah.

The Israelites, who were descendants of Abraham, greatly multiplied, and God was very gracious unto them, formed of them a great nation, and sent the prophet Moses—a holy man to whom God revealed Himself—and commanded him to teach them how to be just and holy, to hate the use of images in worshipping God, and to pray to God (as a man talks in the dark to his friend who is near by but whom he cannot see, yet feeling assured that his friend is near by listening and sympathising)—and gave them laws for the governance of their nation, and ordinances for the pure worship of God, and sacrificial ordinances for redeeming their sinful souls, temporarily, until the Messiah, the Angel of the Lord God, should come and redeem their souls once and for ever.

God also commanded them to be circumcised, that they might be known one to the other to be Jews, and commanded them to keep themselves wholly apart from every other nation, lest they should follow the evil practices of the unteachable idolatrous nations surrounding them, who made images for the eyes to see and to bow down before, as representing the unseen God, uttering prayers, committing the folly of worshipping habitually before vile images, God's abhorrence, as though they were burlesquing the real worshippers of God—not understanding that God has not the shape of a man, is neither male nor female; not understanding that He is on the right hand and on the left, before and behind every one of us. These idolators, therefore, approached very nearly to the senselessness of brutes, and God refused, as before the deluge, to hear the words or accept the worship of wilfully disobedient, idolatrous men; their words in the sight of God being as the barking of a dog, and not as the prayers of pure worshippers.

Notwithstanding the great care of God towards His highly-favoured people the Israelites, they rebelled many times against God—idolatry being their great tempter. The mind of man was constantly striving to set up for itself a spurious form of worship—things which its eyes could see—**for it felt that worship was due to the Creator of all things.** It could not comprehend, owing to the weakness of its intelligence, how the soul could worship without seeing the object, or a representation of the object, to be worshipped.

After Moses died, God sent other holy men, to whom He

revealed Himself, as prophets to His people; but His people, like wayward children, repented and rebelled, by using images in their worship of God and in other idolatrous practices, repented and again rebelled many times; and God satisfied Himself that man was very rebellious, very wicked, and very dull of understanding. God revealed to His servants, the prophets, His fore-ordained plan of redeeming men who learn to understand God. His servants greatly rejoiced, and were enabled to prophecy its fulfilment several hundred years beforehand.

CHAPTER X.

God's Great and Glorious Plan of Redemption.

THE union of one living body with one living soul, the twain forming *one* living man, the man Adam was deemed necessary by God for the furtherance of His great plan for peopling the heaven of the starry firmament, where the Holy Person of God has His dwelling-place; a part of that heaven being prepared for the everlasting habitation of the souls of pardoned men, that God might found a kingdom in heaven for the Messiah, then, as now, a greatly-beloved Angel. Disobedience to God was not the necessary consequence of the creation of man, but God foresaw it might occur; He therefore took the precaution of giving Adam two lives—

    1. The life of his body;
    2. The life of his soul;

the twain forming *one* man, the man Adam. These two lives are the only two lives God has given to Adam, and all his descendants; the countless millions who have ever lived, and may hereafter live, have only these two lives divided betwixt them all, in like manner as a lump of gold may be divided into countless millions of atoms, each atom being as truly gold as the lump itself.

This is the key of the Holy Scriptures.

To every other living creature which God made on the fifth and sixth days of Creation, He gave only *one* life—the life of the body; and to every species of vegetation He made on the third day of Creation, He gave only one life. God on the first six days of creation finished all that has been made, and has made nothing since. He finished the creation in six days; but God contrived that there should be successive generations.

The purpose of God in giving only one living body and one living soul betwixt all mankind was, that in the event of Adam becoming unholy through the passions of his body, God might punish man's temporal body with annihilation, but save his everlasting soul through the mediation of the Messiah, God's foreordained future King in heaven, whose Angel-spirit should in due time be brought out of heaven, and be united to a living body, born out of a pure virgin—the germ of which living body God made at the same time that He made the living body of Adam, but which was kept in abeyance until the time for the advent of the Messiah upon earth should fully come.

The spirit of the angel and the living body born out of the pure virgin, constituting the Messiah Christ who should live as man—as truly man as the man Adam—living a perfectly holy life, and in consequence of the perfect holiness of His living body as well as that of His living soul, be entitled to live for ever with God in heaven, in like manner as the living body and the living soul of Adam would have been entitled to live for ever with God in heaven, if Adam had not introduced sin into the world. Nevertheless, the Holy Messiah should, of His own free will, not in any way being coerced, consent to forfeit the life of His body to satisfy the holy justice of God, which is life for life, so that the punishment of death should be inflicted upon the living body of the Messiah, that the curse wherewith God cursed Adam for his great transgression might be removed. Thus should the Messiah win his Kingship, and thus God, having satisfied his own Divine justice, be enabled to forgive the sin of Adam and of all His descendants who performed the holy act of worshipping God purely, having faith; the Holy Spirit of God then carrying their pardoned souls, upon the death of their body, into the kingdom of heaven prepared for them before the commencement of creation; a large measure of the Holy Spirit of God being added to each minute soul in heaven, thereby giving each the high intelligence of a holy angel, fitting them to be worthy subjects of their Saviour and King, Jesus Christ the Messiah.

This is the mighty plan of God, as revealed in the Holy Scriptures.

CHAPTER XI.

The Messiah.

THE time appointed by God for the coming of the Angel upon earth was about 4000 years after the fall of the man Adam. God had taught the God-fearing Israelites to sacrifice upon altars, the altar sacrifice imputing righteousness as an act of obedience to God of those who sacrificed, showing by their obedience in this respect, that they were teachable, and God pardoned their sins provisionally.

During those 4000 years, the souls of human dead, the pardoned and the unpardoned, were asleep, waiting for the establishment of the Messiah's Kingdom in heaven—the Angel not yet having won his Kingship, being not yet born into the world as man. When the time appointed by God had fully come, as foretold by the prophets, the Holy Spirit of God took the germ of living flesh and blood which He made when He made Adam—and which He had kept in reserve—and placed it in the womb of the pure Virgin Mary, where it was developed and grew; and at the instant of its birth into the world the Holy Spirit of God brought out of heaven the experienced living soul of the Angel—a large soul deeply engraven with remembrances of God and of heaven—and enshrined it in the living flesh and blood, and thus the infant Jesus Christ, the long promised Messiah, was born into the world, having, like all the children of men,

    1. The life of his flesh and blood,
    2. The life of his angel spirit.

The *whole* being of the angel was concentrated in the person of the child Jesus, no portion of the angel being elsewhere, so that, like the man Adam before the great transgression, the Messiah was nothing else than an angel of earth, having, for the purpose of carrying out the plan of his God, wholly given up his position as an angel in heaven temporarily to become a mere man, like unto Adam.

The child Jesus derived his flesh and blood from his mother, the pure Virgin Mary, but not the life thereof, for the life was in the germ which God made when He also made the flesh and blood of Adam; therefore, the child Jesus was born perfectly free from sin, the mother merely nourishing and maturing the living germ which the Holy Spirit of God placed within her womb. The child inherited none of the sin of Adam, for what mankind inherit is inherited from the father and not from the mother—the mother merely nourishing and maturing the life within her womb—therefore, the child Jesus was born as perfectly free from sin as Adam when God created him. God was the only Father of the child Christ as God was the only Father of Adam, descended through his mother from David, yet he inherited nothing from David.

The angels of heaven are sons of God, whereas the pardoned souls of men are *adopted* sons of God—the angel Christ being born into the world out of a woman, the only angel thus born, is therefore the only born Son of God, the Holy Scriptures thus distinguishing him from all the other angels of heaven.

The infant Jesus grew into childhood, into boyhood, and into manhood in all respects as man, and like Adam was nothing more than man; was tempted by the world and by his own passions, as men are tempted; suffered hunger and thirst as men suffer; lived a life of perfect obedience to God in all things; would have no will of his own; made God's will his will; all that God commanded him to say or do, that he said and did, so that what he said was as though God Himself spoke, as though the wisdom of God was manifest in the flesh and visible to the eyes of men.

When Jesus had attained the age ordained by Moses for the assumption of the priesthood, he taught the Israelites that He was the long promised Messiah, the Deliverer of the souls of men; but they, believing the traditions of their false prophets, supposed that the Messiah would reign, not in heaven, but upon earth in great glory, as visible King of the Jews, subduing all nations under Him; they therefore were disappointed, disbelieved Him, were angry and sought to kill Him.

When the time appointed by God had fully come, God permitted the Israelites violently to take hold of the Messiah and mock and scourge Him, and to nail Him cruelly as a culprit ignominiously upon a cross (as the prophets had foretold many hundred years beforehand), thus unwittingly sacrificing the Lamb of God; and while upon the cross the Holy Spirit of God placed upon His body the great sin of Adam. The Messiah was suffering death in the stead of the soul of Adam, thereby rendering Him unholy in the sight of God, like as the lambs sacrificed upon the Jewish altars were unholy, and, therefore, annihilated by being burnt—an unholy state which anguished the holy soul of Christ throughout His earthly life, Christ foreseeing this dreadful cup of bitterness. For three days His body bore that great sin while on the cross and while in the tomb. For three days God and the holy angels in heaven mourned in anguish, for, while on the cross and while in the tomb, the only born Son of God, our kind Deliverer, was impure and unholy in the sight of God, and His eyes were averted from him.

When the allotted time of three days had passed, God removed quickly the curse of another's unholiness from the body of His victorious beloved Son, and carrying Him tenderly into heaven, there placed him upon God's throne on the right hand of God, the place of highest honour next to God, and appointed him Judge in heaven over the souls of all men, the King of pardoned souls, their High Priest, their Deliverer-Almighty to save the true worshippers of God.

The sacrificial death of the Messiah did not save the souls of men, the evil and the good; it simply removed the curse of God which rested upon the soul of Adam through his great transgression. By the sacrificial death of the Messiah the holy justice of God being satisfied of life for life, God is enabled to pardon the sins of all who truly worship Him, repenting of their past misdeeds; therefore the pardoned are carried into heaven not by their own merits, but through the mediatory death of the Messiah.

So long as the curse rested upon man, God was very angry with man, His holy justice being unsatisfied; but through the sacrificial death of Christ the curse and anger of God are removed from man, and His love is turned towards us as before the fall of Adam; therefore Scripture calls Christ Emmanuel (God with us), for it is through his mediatory death that the anger of God is turned into great love for us. Christ is the Alpha and Omega, the first and the last of all God's ransoms, because all-sufficient for the purpose.

Upon this rock (these immutable facts) the kingdom of Christ in heaven, now invisible to us, is founded, whereof his visible Christian Church is part. His earthly subjects form his Church upon earth, which is his kingdom upon earth, he being the sole head of all, the only High Priest of God.

When the risen Christ had been carried by the Holy Spirit of God into heaven, and placed upon the throne of God, at the right hand of God, in the highest place of honour next to God, then the newly-appointed King of Heaven (as God's High Priest, and as God's Judge of all men) caused the souls of all the dead men which had been asleep to come forth for judgment, God's appointed Judge being now ready to reward and to punish. The judgment was awarded; those who died in their sins were judged unworthy to enter heaven, and were, therefore, sent into perdition—sons of perdition—but the pardoned were carried very tenderly and lovingly into heaven by the Holy Spirit of God, being thoroughly purified by the sacrificial death of the Messiah, a holy army of angels, the first-fruits of God's love for man. Thereafter as mankind died, their souls were judged and at once carried tenderly by the Holy Spirit of God into heaven, or sent into perdition.

God has not abdicated His Godhead, neither is He changed, neither has Christ become God—he is still an angel, but the holiest angel in heaven. God has ordained that all men should bow the knee at the name of our Saviour Jesus Christ. It is as the risen Christ, the vanquisher of Sin, the King and Saviour of the pardoned souls of men, the beloved Son of God, sitting upon the right hand of God, upon God's throne, and upon the throne of His kingdom—as our great Friend, that the Saviour is to be worshipped—and not to be worshipped as the man Christ; for while man, neither his mother nor his disciples, who believed in his Messiahship, worshipped him; he had not accomplished his mission, and was simply man—an unholy man while hanging on the cross by reason of the great transgression of Adam, which God there placed upon him. Christ is the King of that portion of the heavens set apart by God as the habitation of the ransomed souls of men, their King, and Lord. The ransomed souls of men in heaven are not men, but angels of the kingdom of Christ.

The life of the body of Christ was sacrificed, slain to save the life of the soul of Adam, not the life of Adam's body, for God condemned that to die for ever, so that Christ laid down one life, not two lives. The thief upon the cross had the sins of his soul pardoned because he repentantly worshipped God, believing in the Messiahship of Christ, although only with his latest breath, but, for the sins of his body, his body was allowed to die and become corrupt, and eaten of worms, and finally to become dust of the earth; in like manner the body of every man is annihilated for ever.

The Holy Spirit of God telegraphs, as it were, to heaven as instantaneously as the touch upon a man's foot is communicated to his head, the prayers of mankind to God and to His Son; but to no other being, for prayer to any other being is an unholy act, an act of superstitious folly, exhibiting faithlessness towards God and towards His Son.

These are the true doctrines as taught in the Holy Scriptures by Christ and by his disciples.

At no time since the creation of Adam, was man so wilfully blind, so cruel as when Christ was upon earth. This God foreknew; therefore, this was the time appointed for the advent of His beloved Son the Messiah, upon earth, because it was necessary for the souls of God-fearing men that they should be pardoned through the *violent* death of the body of Christ, a death which should not proceed from accident, but be purposely slain as a criminal suffering punishment; and it was necessary that Christ should be perfectly holy and therefore estimable, and that he should fully exhibit his credentials before multitudes of men to show that he was really the long-promised Messiah by performing miracles. Men in all other ages, before and after, would have honoured Christ for his holiness, and would have believed in his Messiahship, and therefore would not have desired to harm him, and so, by not slaying him, have thwarted the design of God: this God foreknew, and that the Israelites living in the time of Christ were the only men of all mankind before and after who would have slain the Just One; therefore God permitted them to slay him that they might, unwittingly, further God's plan of redeeming mankind, through the violent death of the body of Christ.

Therefore the Most High God waited for nearly 4000 years.

CHRIST IS COMING

CHRIST IS COMING.

PART IV.

THE HOLY TEACHINGS OF GOD.

CHAPTER I.

The Unity of the Person of God.

THE Holy Scriptures teach that God is *one* Holy Being, as distinct in Person from the Messiah as the person of a human father is distinct from that of his son; therefore the unity of the Person of God is the *foundation* doctrine of the true Church of Christ.

The Messiah, Christ, while upon earth was simply a man—a man like to Moses, and like to every man—born to be a man, that he might as man succeed in passing through an allotted term of life upon earth as a perfectly holy man, accomplishing thereby what Adam failed to do—and that as man he might be able to suffer the death of his body, suffering that punishment as a transgressor against God, in the stead of Adam, the real transgressor; the whole being of the before angel Christ was concentrated in the man Christ, no portion of himself being elsewhere. Whereas only the Holy Person of God is concentrated in heaven, but the residue of His Holy Self, His Holy Spirit, the invisible cloud, is diffused everywhere beyond; and all the angels, and Christ our Messiah, the heavens, the starry skies, and all within them move in that living cloud, like as the fishes of the sea move in the waters of the sea.

Christ having succeeded in his mission upon earth, and being by God exalted to be the King, Lord, and sole Judge in heaven over the souls of those he has ransomed, is almighty to save the souls of his faithful followers, through the almighty power of God, whose almighty power would be exercised on behalf of Christ, the Judge appointed by God. Christ having the power to admit into heaven, or to refuse, is as though he were God, for God would carry out his judgment. Yet Christ is not God. The Messiah is like unto an earthly judge, whose just decree would be enforced by the whole power of the nation; yet the judge is not the nation, nor independently of the nation, has he any power. So the power of Christ is wholly derived from the almighty power of his God, who also is the God of all things.

The Holy Person of God, whose dwelling-place is in the heaven of heavens, is sometimes called the *Word*, because He is the primal source of all spiritual knowledge. The Holy Spirit of God, the living invisible cloud, which is everywhere throughout space, being part of God (like as the wings of a bird are part of the bird), is also sometimes called the *Word*. The Messiah Christ is also sometimes called the *Word*, because he was an angel in heaven before he became man, and revealed greatly more than any other prophet the holy plan of God. The Holy Scriptures are also called the *Word*, because they are the voice of God.

The risen Christ is sometimes called " Everlasting Father;" because, as no unpardoned child of Adam can enter heaven, his children, when pardoned, are no longer the children of Adam, but become the adopted children of Christ, their ranson; eventually entering heaven to live everlastingly with him; therefore Christ is sometimes called their everlasting father—thus the redeemed have two spiritual fathers.

1. God the Creator, the *one* God, the Father of ourselves and of Christ.
2. Christ our King, our Purchaser and Judge, who receives us into his heavenly kingdom as his adopted children.

The Messiah was not our father by adoption, until we prayed to God for pardon, through the great atonement of Christ, whereas God is the Father of the holy and the wicked, the birds of the air, the fishes of the waters, and of all things, because He is their Creator.

Spurious churches have long been bewildering themselves with the foolish and unscriptual doctrine, that a *Trinity of Persons constitute the One God,*—a pagan doctrine forced upon the ignorant people in early Christian times against their common sense, at an epoch when superstition, false legends, and nonsense everywhere were rife,—the spurious priests miscalling their great credulity " Faith," thereby deceiving the well-disposed into giving blind credence and blindly accepting as the foundation of their Christianity the monstrous lie—that *Three Persons constitute the One God.*

How is this great error known to be untrue ?

1. It is more in accordance with the absurd mythology of the Greeks and Romans living in the days of the early Christians, many of whom were Greeks and Romans, than with the common sense of mankind.

2. God has many times declared that there is no other God than Himself.
3. The Scriptures nowhere mention a *Trinity* of persons as constituting *One* God.
4. The absurd doctrine was utterly unknown to the Israelites before the crucifixion, and to the twelve Apostles.
5. The utterance of the Prophets concerning the Messiah alluded to him as a holy being, wholly distinct in person from God.
6. The blessed mother of Christ, her husband Joseph, and the Apostles, although believing that Christ was truly the long-promised Messiah, accounted him in accordance with the prophecies as an angel who came from heaven, and being born out of the Virgin Mary became man, who through God's almighty power, in some way (inexplicable to them until after the resurrection) would save the souls of mankind from being shut out everlastingly from heaven. After the resurrection they fully comprehended, through the teachings of Christ, the mighty plan of God, and clearly understood that his birth out of a pure virgin, his attempted destruction by Herod, the flight of his mother and Joseph with him into Egypt, his great wisdom, his teaching, his great and many miracles, the testimony of John the Baptist, his peculiar public entry into Jerusalem, his betrayal, his crucifixon, his resurrection, the testimony of the angels at his tomb, and his teachings after his resurrection, were in exact accordance with the prophecies concerning the Messiah. Being convinced that he was really the long-promised Messiah they deeply reverenced him as the Messiah,

but did not worship him as they worshipped God—they taught the people after the ascension of Christ, that when upon earth with them he was simply a man like to themselves, giving him the highly reverential spiritual name of Lord; but giving to his God alone the far higher reverential name of God.

7. The utterances of the Apostles, which speak of God and of Christ as two distinct holy beings—the son not equal in power to his Father, but subservient to his Father in all things, the son so obedient as to have no will of his own, but accepting the will of his Father as his own will.

8. The utterances of Christ himself, who ever spoke of God as a Holy Being, wholly distinct from himself, teaching his disciples and the people to pray to God his Father, beseeching Him, praising Him, singing to Him, and giving Him thanks, never accounting himself to be God—plainly saying that God is greater than himself, but calling himself the son of God.

The unwise, idolatrous, early Christian priests, in their admiration of Christ, exalted him in their imagination to be God Himself, forgetting the Creator God, and exalting in their foolish imagination his blessed mother as the mother of God—folly that has been widely perpetuated down to these days. Oh, foolish churches, how great has been your folly, how widely you have departed from the truth; therefore how little you have been able to cope with the wicked heart of man!

In like manner as the Israelites, from the crucifixion down to these days, have erred in disbelieving the Messiahship of Christ, so the spurious Churches have, during many ages, exalted Christ in their imagination to be God. The Israelites and the spurious churches being equal in their great error—the one refusing to acknowledge him as the long promised Messiah, the other exalting him in their imagination as being the Messiah, the Holy Ghost, and God the Creator also; the Israelites refusing to give any glory to Christ, the spurious Churches madly rushing, in their ancient antagonism towards the Jews, to the opposite extreme, by robbing, in their imagination, God the Creator of His Glory, and giving all glory to the Messiah, to the great grief of the Messiah.

Now clearly understand, oh ye nations of the whole world! it was not God who was born out of the Virgin Mary, and who was crucified, but the before holy angel Christ—understand this, and the Holy Scriptures will be plain to your comprehension— Christians have erred greatly during so many generations, in like manner as the followers of Mahomet and of Buddah have erred—errors that were carelessly accepted by powerful rulers, evil and ignorant, and forced upon the priests and the people, generation after generation. The time is at hand, even knocking at the door, when your understanding shall be made clear, and neither the professing followers of Christ, nor of Buddah, nor of Mahomet, nor the unwise of other sects, will continue in their many errors.

Evidences of the unity of God, and that Christ is not God but the son of God—two Holy Beings, whose persons are as distinct as the person of a human father is distinct from that of his son.

The Record of the Prophets.

The Psalms.

The Record of God concerning Moses.

1. "And he (Aaron) shall be thy spokesman unto the people; and he shall be, even he, shall be to thee, instead of a mouth, and thou (Moses) shalt be to him *instead of God.*"
2. "And the Lord said unto Moses, See, I have made thee *as a God to Pharaoh;* and Aaron thy brother shall be thy prophet; thou shalt speak all that I command thee, and Aaron thy brother shall speak unto Pharaoh."

The Record of Moses.

1. "The Lord thy God will raise up unto thee a prophet in the midst of thee, of thy brethren, like unto me, and unto him shall ye hearken."

The Record of God.

1. "Behold *my servant* whom I have chosen, in whom my soul is well pleased, I will put my spirit upon him, and he shall shew judgment unto the Gentiles."
2. "And lo! a voice from heaven, saying, This is my beloved *son*, in whom I am well pleased."
3. "Fear not, Mary, for behold thou shalt conceive in thy womb and bring forth a son, and shalt call his name Jesus; he shall be great, and shall be called the *Son* of the Highest; and the Lord God shall give unto him the throne of his father David, and he shall reign over the house of Jacob for ever and ever, and of his kingdom there shall be no end. The Holy Ghost shall come upon thee, and the power of the highest shall overshadow thee, therefore that holy thing which shall be born of thee shall be called the *Son* of God, for with God nothing shall be impossible."

The Record of John the Baptist.

1. "The next day John seeing Jesus coming unto him, saith, Behold the *Lamb* of God, which taketh away the sin of the world."
2. "John (the Baptist) bare witness of Christ, saying, This is he of whom I spake, he that cometh after me is preferred before me, for he was (in existence) before me."

The Record of Christ.

1. "I came down from heaven, not to do mine own will, but the will of Him that sent me."
2. "My doctrine is not mine, but His that sent me."
3. "I must work the works (carry out the plan) of Him that sent me."
4. "I am only *sent* unto the lost sheep of the house of Israel."
5. "I came forth from the Father, and am come into the world; again I leave the world and go to the Father."
6. "*I can of mine own self do nothing*, as I hear I judge, and my judgment is just because I seek not mine own will, but the will of the Father which sent me."
7. "Whoever shall do the will of my Father which is in *heaven*, the same is *my brother, and sister, and mother*."
8. "The first of all the commandments is, The Lord *our* God is *one* Lord."
9. "Blessed are the pure in heart, for they shall see God."
10. "Why callest thou *me* good, there is none good but God."
11. "No man hath seen God at any time, the only begotten son, which is in the confidence of the Father, he has declared Him."
12. "The Father himself which hath *sent* me, hath borne witness of me; *ye have neither heard His voice at any time, nor seen His shape*."
13. "*I am come in my Father's name*, and ye receive me not."
14. "I have greater witnesses than John (the Baptist), the works which the Father hath given me to accomplish the same works I do, they bear witness of me that the Father hath *sent* me."
15. "God so loved the world that He gave His only begotten son, that whoso believeth in him should not perish but have everlasting life, for God *sent* not His son into the world to condemn the world, but that the world through him might be saved."
16. "*I have not spoken of myself*, but the Father which sent me, He gave me commandment what I should say; whatsoever I speak, therefore, even as the Father *said unto me* so I speak."
17. "Let your (spiritual) light so shine before men, that they may see your good works and glorify your *Father which is in heaven*."
18. "Be ye therefore perfect, as *your Father which is in heaven* is perfect."
19. "Take heed that ye do not your alms before men, to be seen of them, otherwise ye have no reward of *your Father which is in heaven*."
20. "Whoever therefore shall confess me before men, him will I confess *before my Father which is in heaven*. He that receiveth me, receiveth Him that *sent* me."

21. "Take heed that ye despise not one of these little ones, for I say unto you that in heaven their angels do *always behold the face of my Father which is in heaven.*"

22. "To sit on my right hand, and on my left hand, is *not mine,* but it shall be given to them for whom it is prepared by *my Father.*"

23. "But whom say ye that I am? And Simon Peter answered and said Thou art the Christ, *the Son of the living God.* And Jesus answered, and said unto him, Blessed art thou, Simon Barjona, for flesh and blood have not revealed it unto thee, but my *Father which is in heaven.*"

24. "If ye then being evil know how to give good gifts to your children, how much more shall *your Father which is in heaven* give good things to them that ask Him. Not every one that saith unto me, Lord, Lord, shall enter into the kingdom of heaven."

25. "Of that day and hour knoweth no man, no not the angels, *neither the Son, but the Father.*"

26. "*The Father loveth the Son, and hath given all things into his hand* (relating to mankind)."

27. "Verily, verily, I say unto you, he that receiveth whomsoever I send (the twelve apostles), receiveth me; and he that receiveth me receiveth Him that *sent* me."

28. "Whoever, therefore, shall acknowledge me before men, him will I acknowledge *before my Father which is in heaven;* but whomsoever shall deny me before men. him also will I deny *before my Father which is in heaven.*"

29. "As the Father knoweth me, even so know I the Father; and I lay down my life for the sheep, therefore *doth my Father love me,* because I lay down my life, that I might take it again—no man taketh it from me, but I lay it down myself; I have power (as a man without sin) to lay it down, and I have power (as a man without sin) to take it again (the perfect holiness of Christ entitled him to live for ever without tasting death); this commandment *have I received from my Father.* Then came the Jews round about him, and said unto him, How long dost thou make us to doubt? If thou be the Christ, tell us plainly. And Jesus answered, I told you and you believed me not: the works that *I do in my Father's name* they bear witness of me, but ye believed not, because ye are not of my sheep; as I said unto you, my sheep hear my voice (comprehend me), and I know them, and they follow me, and I give unto them eternal life; and they shall never perish, neither shall any man pluck them out of my hand; *my Father which gave*

them to me is greater than all, and no man is able to pluck them out of my Father's hand, I and my Father are one : then the Jews took up stones again to stone him (the Jews misunderstood the meaning of Christ's words, 'I and my Father are one ;' he meant that God would exercise His power in behalf of Christ, and in behalf of his followers). Jesus answered them, Many good works have I showed you *from my Father*, for which of these good works do ye stone me. Say ye of him whom *the Father hath sanctified and sent* into the world, thou blasphemest, because I said I am the *Son of God?* If I do not the works of my Father (the things prophecied), believe me not, but if I do, though ye believe not me, believe the works, that ye may know and believe that the Father (the Holy Spirit of God) *is in me and I in him;* and Jesus *lifted up his eyes* and said, *Father, I thank thee that thou hast heard me,* I knew that *thou hearest me always.*"

30. "And I appoint unto you a kingdom, as *my Father hath* appointed unto me."
31. "Hereafter shall the Son of Man sit on the *right hand* of the power of God."
32. "For *the Father judgeth no man*, but hath committed all judgment unto the Son, that all men should know the Son, even as they know (by worship) the Father, for as the Father hath life eternal in himself, so hath *he given* to his Son to have everlasting life in himself (like as angels have everlasting life in themselves)."
33. "And yet if I judge my judgment is true, for I am not *alone*, but I and the Father that *sent* me (are two witnesses) ; it is written in your law that the testimony of two witnesses is to be received. *I am one* that beareth witness of myself, *and* the Father that sent me beareth witness (also). Ye are from beneath (of the earth), I am from above (from heaven). Ye are of this world, I am not of this world : I have many things to say and to communicate to you, but he that sent me is true, and I speak to the world those things that *I have heard of Him.* They understood not that he spake to them of the Father. Then said Jesus unto them, when ye (the children of Adam) have lifted up the Son of Man (crucified him high upon the cross), then shall ye know that I am he (the Christ as prophesied), and that *I do nothing of myself*, but as my father hath *taught me.* I speak these things, and He that sent me is with me, the Father (the Holy Spirit of God) hath not left me alone (does not shrink from me) ; for I do always those things that please Him, and now you seek to kill me, *a man* that hath told you the

truth which *I have heard* of God. If God were your Father you would love me, for I proceeded forth (out of heaven) and came from God; neither came I myself (not in accordance with any plan of mine), but *He sent me:* if I honour myself, my honour is nothing, *it is the Father that honoureth me,* of whom ye say, He is your God. Verily, verily, I say unto you, before Abraham was (born) I existed."

35. "All things are delivered unto me by my Father, and no man knoweth the Son (fully) but the Father, neither knoweth any man the Father (fully) save the Son, and he to whomsoever the Son will reveal Him."

36. "If ye loved me ye would rejoice, because I said, I go unto the Father, *for my Father is greater than I.*"

37. "Let not your heart be troubled; ye (already) believe in God, believe also in me. In my Father's house (heaven) are many mansions (heavens), I go to prepare a place for you. I am the way, the truth, and the life, no man cometh unto the Father, but by me. If ye had known me, ye should have known my Father also; and from henceforth ye have known Him, and have seen Him (for Christ represented God, as an ambassador represents his king). Philip saith unto him, Lord, shew us the Father, and it sufficeth us? Jesus saith unto him, Have I been so long with you, and yet hast thou not known me, Philip (that I was truly God's ambassador)? he that hath seen me hath seen the Father, and how sayest thou shew us the Father; believest thou not that I am in the (Holy Spirit of the) Father, and *ye in me* and *I in you*. He that loveth me not, keepeth not my sayings, and the *word* (revelation) which ye hear *is not mine, but the Father's which sent me.*"

38. "But that the world may know that *I love the Father,* and as the Father gave me commandment, so I do."

39. "Jesus *prayed,* I thank thee, O Father, Lord of heaven and earth, because thou hast hid these things from the wise and prudent, and hast revealed them unto babes; even so Father, for so it seemeth good in thy sight."

40. "And Jesus was withdrawn from them about a stone's cast, and *kneeled down and prayed.*"

41. "Jesus went a little further, and *fell on his face and prayed;* saying, O my Father, if it be possible, let this cup pass from me; nevertheless, *not as I will but as thou wilt.*"

42. "I will *pray* the Father, and he shall give you another Comforter, that he may abide with you for ever, even the Spirit of Truth (conviction)."

43. " But when the Comforter is come, whom I will send unto you from the Father, even the Spirit of Truth, which proceedeth from the Father, he shall testify of me ; and ye also shall bear witness, because ye have been with me from the beginning (of Christ's teaching)."

44. " Jesus *prays*, Father I will that they also (Christ's followers) whom thou hast given me may be with me (in heaven) where I go, that they may behold the glory which *thou hast given me;* for thou lovedst me before the foundation (creation) of the world."

45. " Thinkest thou that I cannot now *pray* to my Father, and he will give me more than twelve legions of angels?"

46. " Father, save me from this hour, but for this cause came I into this hour. Father, glorify thy name. Then there came a voice from heaven, saying, I have both glorified it and will glorify it again."

47. " *My God, my God, why hast thou forsaken me !*"

48. " *Into thy hands I commend my spirit* ; after he had uttered these words Jesus gave up the ghost (died)."

49. "And Jesus came and spake unto them (after his resurrection from the tomb), saying, All power *is given* unto me in heaven (that portion set aside for the pardoned souls of men) and in earth, go ye, therefore, teach all nations, baptizing them in the name of the Father, and of the Son, and of the Holy Ghost (the Holy Scriptures)."

50. " I ascend unto my FATHER AND YOUR FATHER, to *my God and your God*."

The Record of St. Mark.

1. " The beginning of the gospel of Jesus Christ the *Son of God*."

2. " So then after the Lord had spoken unto them, he was received up into heaven, and sat *on the right hand of God*."

The Record of St. Luke.

1. "And behold it came to pass, while he blessed them, he was parted from them, and *carried* into heaven."

The Record of St. Stephen.

1. " Behold, I see the heavens opened, and the *Son of Man standing on the right hand of God*."

The Record of St. James.
1. "James, a servant of God, *and* of the Lord Jesus Christ."

The Record of St. Peter.
1. "Ye men of Israel, hear these words, Jesus of Nazareth, *a man approved of God* among you by miracles and wonders and signs, *which God did by him* in the midst of you, as ye yourselves also know ; him, being delivered by the determinate counsel and foreknowledge of God, ye have taken, and by wicked hands have crucified and slain, *whom God hath raised up*, having loosed the pains of death."
2. "*This Jesus hath God raised up*, whereof we (his disciples) are all witnesses ; therefore being by the right hand of God exalted."
3. "Therefore let all the house of Israel know assuredly, *that God hath made that same Jesus*, whom ye have crucified, both Lord and Christ."
4. "The God of Abraham, and of Isaac, and of Jacob, the God of our father *hath glorified His son Jesus*."
5. "And killed the prince of life, *whom God hath raised from the dead*, whereof we are witnesses."
6. "But those things which God had shewed by the mouth of all His prophets that Christ should suffer."
7. "For Moses truly said unto the fathers, *A prophet shall the Lord your God raise up unto you, like unto me.*"
8. "Be it known unto you all, and to all the people of Israel, that by the name of Jesus Christ of Nazareth, whom ye crucified, *whom God raised from the dead.*"
9. "*The God of our fathers raised up Jesus*, whom ye slew and hanged ; *him hath God exalted* with His right hand to be *a Prince and Saviour*, for to give repentance to Israel and forgiveness of sins."
10. "How *God anointed Jesus of Nazareth with the Holy Ghost*, and with power, who went about doing good, and healing all that were oppressed of the devil ; *for God was with him--him God raised up* the third day, and showed him openly, and he (Christ) commanded us to preach unto the people, and to testify that it was he which was *ordained of God*, to be the judge of quick and dead : to him gave all the prophets witness that through his name whosoever believeth in him shall receive remission of sins."

11. " Blessed be *the God and Father of our Lord Jesus Christ*."
12. " But with the precious blood of Christ, as of a lamb without blemish and without spot, who verily was fore-ordained before the foundation of the world, but was manifest in these last times for you, who by him do believe *in God that raised him up* from the dead and *gave him* glory."
13. " For Christ also hath once suffered for sins, the just for the unjust, *that he might bring us to God*."
14. " Thou art the Christ, *the Son* of the living God."

The Record of St. Paul.

1. " The *God of our Lord Jesus Christ*."
2. " And be ye kind one to another, tender-hearted; forgiving one another, *as God for Christ's sake* hath forgiven you."
3. " Giving thanks always for all things *unto God the Father*, in the name of *our Lord Jesus Christ*."
4. " Wherefore God also hath highly exalted him, and given him a name which is above every name, that at the name of Jesus every knee should bow, and that every tongue should confess that Jesus is Lord, to the Glory of God the Father."
5. " Grace, mercy, and peace, from God our Father, *and* Jesus Christ our Lord."
6. " For there is *one* God and *one* Mediator *between* God and man, the *man* Jesus Christ, who gave himself a ransom for all."
7. " I charge thee, before God and the Lord Jesus Christ."
8. " But after that the kindness and love of *God our Saviour* toward man appeared, which he shed on us so abundantly, *through Jesus Christ our Saviour*."
9. " God, who at sundry times and in divers manners, spake in time past unto the fathers by the prophets, hath in these last days spoken unto us *by His Son*, whom He hath appointed heir of all things, by (for) whom also He made the worlds; who being the express image of His person (by reason of his holiness), and upholding all things by the word of His power, when he (Christ), had by himself purged our sins, sat down on the right hand of the Majesty on high (God), *being made so much better than the angels*, as he hath by inheritance (through his redemption of obtained a more excellent name than they."

10. "But we see Jesus, *who was made a little lower than the angels*, for the suffering of death, that he, by the grace of God, should taste death for every man."

11. "And to make all men see what is the fellowship of the mystery, which from the beginning of the world hath been hid in God, who hath created all things by (for) Jesus Christ."

12. "One Lord (Christ), one faith, one baptism, *one* God and Father of all, who *is above all*, and through all, and in you all."

13. "Giving thanks unto the Father, which has made us meet to be partakers of the inheritance of the saints in light, who hath delivered us from the power of darkness, and hath translated us into the kingdom of *His dear Son*, in whom we have redemption through his blood, even the forgiveness of sins; who is the image of the invisible God, the first-born (the most exalted) of every living creature. For by Him (God) were all things created that are in heaven, and that are in earth, visible and invisible, whether thrones, or dominions, or principalities, or powers, all things were created by Him (God), and for him (Christ), and he before all things, and by (for) him all (created) things consist."

14. "I thank God, *through* Jesus Christ our Lord."

15. "God sending *His own Son* in the likeness of sinful flesh."

16. "And if children, then heirs of God, *and joint heirs* with Christ."

17. "He that spared not *His Son*, but delivered him up for us all."

18. "It is Christ that died, yea, rather that is risen again, who is even *at the right hand of God*."

19. "If thou shalt confess with thy mouth the Lord Jesus, and shalt believe in thine heart that *God hath raised him* from the dead, thou shalt be saved."

20. "That ye may with one mind and one mouth glorify God, even *the Father of our Lord Jesus Christ*."

21. "Grace be unto you, and peace from God our Father, *and* from the Lord Jesus Christ."

22. "And ye are Christ's, *and* Christ is God's."

23. "But thanks be to God, who giveth us the victory, *through* our Lord Jesus Christ."

24. "Grace be to you, and peace from God our Father, *and* from the Lord Jesus Christ; blessed be God, even the *Father of our Lord Jesus Christ*, the Father of mercies, and the God of all comfort."

25. "Knowing that *He which raised up the Lord Jesus* shall raise up us also *by* Jesus."
26. "For ye are all the children of God by faith in Christ Jesus, for as many of you as have been baptized unto Christ have put on Christ."
27. "But when the fulness of the time was come, *God sent forth his Son*, born of a woman."
28. "Blessed be the *God and Father* of our Lord Jesus Christ."
29. "Of this man's (David) seed hath God, according to his promise, *raised* unto Israel a saviour, Jesus."
30. "Paul, a servant of Jesus Christ, called to be an apostle, separated unto the Gospel of God, which he had promised afore by his prophets in the Holy Scriptures, concerning *His Son* Jesus Christ, our Lord, which was made of the seed of David according to the flesh, and declared to be the *Son* of God with power."
31. "First, I thank my God, *through* Jesus Christ, for you all."
32. "For all have sinned, and come short of the Glory of God, being justified freely by his grace, through the redemption that is in Christ Jesus, *whom God sent forth* to be a propitiation through faith in his blood."
33. "But for us also, to whom it shall be imputed, if we believe on *Him that raised up Jesus* the Lord from the dead."
34. "Therefore, being justified by faith, we have peace with God, *through* our Lord Jesus Christ."
35. "For if when we were enemies we were reconciled to God by the death of *His Son*."
36. "Like as Christ *was raised* up from the dead by the glory of the Father."
37. "Likewise reckon ye also yourselves to be dead indeed unto sin, but alive unto God, *through* Jesus Christ our Lord."
38. "For the wages of sin is death, but the gift of God is eternal life, *through* Jesus Christ our Lord."
39. "Let the mind be in you which was also in Christ, who being in the form of God (by reason of his holiness) thought it no robbery to be equal with God (in that Christ commanded his disciples to baptize all nations in the name of the Father and of the Son), but made himself of no reputation, and took upon himself the form of a servant, and *was made* in the likeness of man, and being found (finding himself) in fashion as a man, he humbled himself, and became obedient unto death, wherefore God also hath highly exalted him."

The Record of St. Jude.

1. "For there are certain men crept in unawares, who were of old ordained to this condemnation, ungodly men, turning the grace of our Lord into lasciviousness, and denying the *only* Lord God *and* our Lord Jesus Christ."
2. "Keep yourselves in the love of God, looking for the mercy of our Lord Jesus Christ unto eternal life."

The Record of St. John.

St. John commences, after the manner of Christ, with a riddle, which afterwards he interprets:

1. "In the beginning (of creation) was the Word (the revealer, Christ), and the Word was (Christ lived) with God, and the Word (the source of all revelation) was God. The same (Christ) was in the beginning (of creation) *with* God. All things were made by Him (God); and without Him was not anything made that was made."
2. "And the Word (Christ) was made flesh, and dwelt among us; and we beheld his glory, as of the only begotten of the Father, full of grace and truth."
3. "*No man hath seen God* at any time; the only begotten Son, which is in the bosom of the Father, he hath declared Him."
4. "That (Christ) which was from the beginning (of creation), which we have heard, which *we have seen with our eyes*, which we have looked upon, and our hands have handled, of the Word of Life (Christ); for the Life was manifested, and we have seen it, and bear witness, and show unto you that eternal life (Christ) *which was with the Father*, and was manifested unto us. And truly our fellowship is with the Father, *and with His Son Jesus* Christ. And these things write we unto you, that your joy may be full. This then is the message we have heard from him, and declare unto you, that God is light, and in Him is no darkness at all. If we walk in the light, as He is in the light, we have fellowship one with another, and the blood of Jesus Christ *His Son* cleanseth us from all sin."
5. "And if any man sin, we have an advocate *with* the Father, Jesus Christ the righteous."

6. "And this is His commandment, that we should believe on the name of *His Son* Jesus Christ."

7. "In this was manifested the love of God towards us, because that God *sent* His only begotten Son into the world, that we might live through him. Herein is love, not that we loved God, but that He loved us, and *sent His Son* to be the propitiation for our sins. *No man hath seen God* at any time. And we have seen and do testify that the Father *sent the Son* to be the saviour of the world. Whosoever shall *confess that Jesus is the Son of God*, God dwelleth in him, and he in God."

8. "Whosoever believeth that Jesus is the Christ, is born of God."

9. "Who is he that overcometh the world, but he that believeth that Jesus is the Son of God? There are three that bear record in heaven, the Father, the Word (Christ), and the Holy Ghost (the Holy Scriptures); these three are one (agree in testimony). And this is the record (testimony) that God has given to us eternal life, and this life is in (through) His Son."

10. "And we know that the Son of God is come, and hath given us an understanding, that we may know him that is true; and we are in him that is true, even in *His Son* Jesus Christ."

11. "Grace be with you, mercy, and peace, from God the Father, *and* from the Lord Jesus Christ, *the Son of the Father*."

12. "But Thomas, one of the twelve, was not with them when (the risen) Jesus came, the other disciples therefore said unto him, We have seen the Lord; but he said unto them, Except I shall see in his hands the print of the nails, and put my finger into the print of the nails, and thrust my hands into his side, I will not believe. And after eight days again his disciples were within, and Thomas with them; then came Jesus—the door being shut—and stood in the midst, and said, Peace be unto you; then said he to Thomas Reach hither thy finger and behold my hands, and reach hither thy hand, and thrust it into my side, and be not faithless, but believing; and Thomas answered and said unto him, My Lord and (the ejaculation) my God! And many other signs truly did Jesus in the presence of his disciples, which are not written, that ye might believe that Jesus is the Christ, *the Son of God*."

13. "And he shewed me a pure river of water, clear as crystal, proceeding out of the throne of God *and* of the Lamb (Christ). In the midst of the street of it, and on either side of the river, was there the tree of life, which bare twelve manner of fruits, and yielded her fruit every month, and the leaves of the trees are for the heal-

ing of the nations. And there shall be no more curse, but the throne of God *and of the Lamb* shall be in it (heaven), and his servants shall serve him, and they shall see his face, and his (Christ's) name shall be in their foreheads; and there shall be no night there; and they need no candle, neither light of the sun; for the Lord God giveth them light, and they shall reign for ever and ever. And he said unto me, These sayings are faithful and true; and the Lord God of the holy prophets sent His angel to shew unto His servants the things which must shortly be done. Behold, I come quickly; blessed is he that keepeth the sayings of the prophecy of this book. And I John saw these things, and heard them; and when I had heard and seen, *I fell down to worship before the feet of the angel* which shewed me these things. Then saith he unto me, See thou do it not, *for I am thy fellow servant*, and of thy brethren the prophets, and of them which keep the sayings of this book; *worship God*. And he said unto me, Seal not the sayings of the prophecy of this book, for the time is at hand. He that is unjust, let him be unjust still; and he which is filthy, let him be filthy still; and he that is righteous, let him be righteous still; and he that is holy, let him be holy still. And, behold, I come quickly, and my reward is with me, to give every man according as his work shall be. I am Alpha and Omega, the beginning and the end, the first and the last (of all sacrifices). *I, Jesus*, have sent mine angel to testify unto you these things. *I am the root and the offspring* of David, and the bright and morning star."

CHAPTER II.

The Commandments of God.

I. Thou shalt have no other gods but me.
II. Thou shalt not make to thyself any graven image, nor the likeness of anything that is in heaven above, or in the earth beneath, or in the waters; thou shalt not bow down to them, nor worship them, for I, the Lord thy God am a jealous God, visiting

the sins of the fathers upon the children unto the third and fourth generation of them that disobey me and shewing mercy unto them that love me and obey my commandments.

III. Thou shalt not take the name of the Lord thy God in vain, for the Lord will not hold him guiltless that taketh His name in vain.

IV. **Remember that thou keep holy the Sabbath Day· six days shalt** thou labour, and **do all that thou hast to do,** but the seventh day is the Sabbath of the Lord thy God: in it thou shalt do no manner of work, neither thou, nor thy son, nor thy daughter, nor thy man servant, nor thy maid servant, nor thy cattle, nor the stranger that is within thy gates; for in six days the Lord made heaven and earth, the sea, and all within them, and rested the seventh day, wherefore the Lord blessed the seventh day and hallowed it.

V. Honour thy father and thy mother, that thy days may be long in the place which the Lord thy God hath provided for thee.

VI. Thou shalt do no murder.

VII. Thou shalt not commit adultery.

VIII. Thou shalt not steal.

IX. Thou shalt not bear false witness.

X. Thou shalt not covet any man's house, neither shalt thou covet his wife, nor his servant, nor his maid, nor his ox, nor his ass, nor anything that is his.

The Commandment of Christ.

Thou shalt love thy neighbour as thyself.

CHAPTER III.

The Ordinance of the Feast of Unity.

OUR Blessed Lord, on the day of the Jewish Feast of the Passover, a feast of spiritual unity of purpose among the Israelites, knowing that his mediatory death would take place on the morrow, instituted a Feast of Unity, as a sacred ordinance for the future Christian church, which should be to them a bond of union, like as the Jewish Feast of the Passover was a bond of union to the Israelites. The Lord knew that in the hearts of his disciples spiritual ambition lay lurking; he had observed their antagonism for ascendency, and their consequent proneness to separation one from the other, for they were as yet but men learning to understand the mission of Christ. And as were his disciples, so would be his followers after them, all tending to separate one from the other because of the infirmity of their nature; therefore he taught them to cease their strife, and to live unitedly and in the holy bonds of spiritual love one for the other, communing together as members of one holy family, each giving way to the other out of real mutual love, through real love for God. Instancing his own transcendant love for them, and for all mankind, in giving himself to God, as a substitute, for the punishment of death, in the place of Adam, the great transgressor against the holy law of obedience towards God; instancing also that he, an angel of heaven, living there with God and the holy angels of God in greatest happiness, of his own free will, out of his great love for God and for mankind, came down from heaven and became man, suffering distress, both of body and mind, and suffering that terrible thing in the sight of holy angels—death : that dreadful sign of a great punishment for rebellion against God. Instancing thus his great love for mankind, and urgently desired that his disciples, and all his after followers, should concede one to the other for the good of the whole church, and for the good of all mankind; ordaining that the occasional Feast of Unity, after the forthcoming crucifixion, should be a real bond of union to all his true followers. At this sacred feast, his approaching mediatory death, their spiritual consolation, and spiritual unity among his followers, were the great themes of our Blessed Lord.

> "And when the hour was come he sat down, and the twelve disciples with him, and he said unto them, With desire I have desired to eat this Passover with you before I suffer, for I say unto you, I will not eat any more thereof until it (the plan of God) be fulfilled in the kingdom of God."
>
> "As the disciples were eating the Passover, Jesus took the (passover) bread and blessed it, and brake it, and gave it to his disciples, and said, Take, eat, this (pointing to his body) is my body, which is given (to death) for you ; this do *in remembrance* of me, and he took the cup and gave it to them, saying, Drink ye all of it, for (again pointing to his body) this is my blood of the new dispensation, which is (about being) shed for many for the remission of sins ; but, I say unto you, I will not drink henceforth of *this fruit of the vine*, until I drink it new with you in my Father's kingdom."

Mark well, ye nations ! the wine they drank was still wine, and which Christ himself drank ; and the bread mere passover bread, unchanged. Neither the bread nor the wine influenced for good Judas Iscariot in the least, nor prevented strife among the disciples immediately afterwards, as to which of them should be the greatest among them, nor prevented Peter directly after denying his Lord, nor prevented the other disciples seeking safety in flight from the arrested Messiah, although Christ himself blessed the bread and the wine ; evidencing that neither the bread nor the wine had in themselves any spiritual value, like as the roasted lamb and the passover bread in the Jewish Feast of the Passover had in themselves no spiritual value. The spirituality of the feast consisting in the Israelites doing certain things in obedience to an ordinance of God, in commemoration of the great mercy of God towards their forefathers, and therefore towards themselves, who were in their forefathers, in the land of Egypt.

> " And, at the supper, Jesus said, 'A new commandment I give unto you, that ye love one another; as I have loved you, so also do ye love one another; by this shall all men know ye are my disciples, if ye have love one to another.'"

For unless unity of purpose and mutual love bind together his professing followers, they are not of his church; they cannot restrain the wickedness of mankind.

> " Immediately after the supper Jesus went out and prayed, saying, 'Neither pray I for these (his disciples) alone, but for all them which shall believe in me through their word, that they all may be one (church), as thou, Father, art in me and I in thee, that they all may be one in us, that the world may believe that thou hast sent me and the glory (word) which thou hast given me I have given (uttered to) them, that they may be (of) one (mind) even as we are (of) one (mind). I in thee and thou in me, that they may be made perfect in one (unity of spirit) and that the world may know that thou hast sent me and hast loved them as thou hast loved me. Father, I will that they also whom thou hast given me may be with me where I am, that they may behold the glory which thou hast given me, for thou lovedst me before the foundation (creation) of the world. O righteous Father, the world has not comprehended thee, but I have comprehended thee, and these have comprehended that thou hast sent me, and I have declared unto them thy name, and will declare it, that the love wherewith thou hast loved me may be in them, and I (loving remembrance of me) in them.'"

The sacred ordinance of the Feast of Unity is an ordinance of great value in the sight of all the zealous followers of Christ, those staunch believers who are convinced of the truthfulness of the Holy Scriptures, and who therefore strive their uttermost to win souls to Christ. They are the holy workers of the church—the saints of the true Church of Christ; the very salt of the earth; the most estimable of all mankind within the earth; equal in the sight one of the other, because they all are children of God—from whom are selected the spiritual teachers. This sacred ordinance is the very opposite to the nonsensical ordinance of spurious churches, which attribute superstitious virtue to the bread and wine, altogether forgetting that the maintenance of mutual love and unity among his true followers was the great purpose of the Lord in instituting the sacred ordinance. Ye have erred greatly, oh, ye many sects! the Messiah did not say that the passover bread which he himself ate was his body, nor the wine which he himself drank was his blood, but desired them to break bread and drink wine together not as an ordinary meal, to satisfy the appetite, but expressly in remembrance of his mediatory death, urging them to love one another—instancing his own great love for mankind in suffering the terrible punishment of death in their stead. It is neither the bread nor the wine which sanctifies the partakers of the feast, but their mutual spiritual love and zealous unanimity of purpose—it is that which stamps them as the dutiful children of God.

Like as the sacred Feast of the Passover is a commemorative feast to the Israelites, of their escape, so the sacred Feast of Unity is a commemorative feast of our escape through the one great atonement. The Israelites to this day have commemorated their feast purely as in the days of Moses, never dreaming of attaching an idolatrous meaning to it; but not so the spurious churches, to their shame; therefore, these are split into fragments, and there is now no real Feast of Unity, because of the desire of the spurious teachers of the people to glorify themselves in the estimation of the people by impiously and foolishly pretending to work the miracle of converting bread and wine into the real body and blood of Christ. Herein is the root of the many evils which afflict the nations of the whole world, for the nonsense of professing Christians causes them to be powerless in converting the nations to God.

CHAPTER IV.

The Blessed Mother of Christ.

IT was necessary, in furtherance of the mighty plan of God, fore-ordained before the starry skies and this round earth were made, that the angel Christ should come upon earth, and be born of a pure virgin, that he might be born without inheriting sin—for that which is inherited comes from the male, and not from the female—the female of every living creature simply nourishing, developing, and in due time producing, the fruit of her womb, like as the ground nourishes and developes the seed planted in it. It was necessary that the infant Christ should be born perfectly free from sin.

When the appointed time, as declared by the prophets, had fully come, the Holy Spirit of God—the living cloud which is everywhere throughout space—took the germ of living flesh and blood, which God made when He made Adam, and which for about 4000 years He kept in reserve, and placed it in the womb of the pure Virgin Mary, where it was developed, was nourished, and grew; and at the instant of its birth, the Holy

Spirit of God brought out of heaven the living soul of the angel Christ, a soul deeply engraven with remembrances of God and of heaven, and enshrined it in the living flesh and blood that was issuing out of the pure Virgin's womb. Thus was the infant Jesus born into the world, without sin, and having, like all the children of men, two lives—

1. The life of his flesh and blood.
2. The life of his soul.

God being his only Father, like as God is also the only Father of Adam. Thus was Jesus born a child of mankind, and yet not a child of Adam, for naught that was in Jesus was in Adam at any time ; and thus was the Blessed Virgin honoured by being made an instrument, in like manner as Adam, Noah, Abraham, Isaac, Jacob, Moses, Aaron, David, and numerous other holy people recorded in Holy Scripture, were equally blessed instruments in the hands of God.

Christ treated his mother Mary as a loving son treats a loving mother, but declared that all who loved God were his father, mother, sister, and brother, and gently chid the woman who said, "Blessed is the womb that bare thee and the paps which thou hast sucked," by rejoining "Yea rather blessed are they that hear the word of God and act up to it."

The mother of Jesus was the betrothed wife of Joseph, and became the mother of several children by Joseph, who were in all things as other children, not one whit holier born than they. Jesus was the first born of his mother, as it is written, "Joseph knew not his wife till she had brought forth her first born son." Again it is written, "While he yet talked to the people behold his mother and his brothers stood without, desiring to speak with him ; he said unto the people, Who is my mother and who are my brothers?" he stretched forth his hands towards *his disciples* and said, "Behold my mother and my brothers." It is also written, "The Jews enquired one of another, saying, is not his mother called Mary, and his brothers James, and Joses, and Simeon, and Judas, and his sisters are they not all with us. God fore-ordained that the mother of Christ should have children by her husband Joseph, to shew mankind that she was like unto all other women, being simply an instrument of God in furtherance of His holy plan for redeeming the souls of mankind.

Mary was born in sin, like all the other children of Adam, had the passions of women, and was subject, like all the other mothers of Israel, to the Jewish laws of purification, and died an *elderly married woman.* Her body corrupting like as the body of every child of Adam dies and corrupts, by reason of its sinfulness. In all things truly woman, like unto every pious daughter of mankind ; and like them, being pardoned only through the mediatory death of Christ. Moreover, the souls of mankind in heaven have no recollection of the earth, sinful earth ! all remembrances, the evil and the good, being wiped out by death; the soul entering there as it were newly born, not one spirit recognizing another as of earth, but recognizing each other only as children of the living God, and as children of King Jesus. Nevertheless, like as senseless men have made images of a man upon a cross, worshipping them, so have they made images and pictures of a woman, and worship them. Abominations in the sight of God, introduced by the early idolatrous Gentile converts debasing Christianity by allying it with Paganism; imitating the Pagan Ephesians of old, by making for themselves an imaginary Goddess.

At the birth of the infant angel man Christ the blessed mother of Christ was truly a pure virgin ; but afterwards she was no longer a virgin but the mother of several children of Adam, by her husband Joseph. Yet does the spurious sect of the Papacy, for her idolatrous purposes, teach her deceived people the monstrous lie that she had no other child but Jesus, and died a virgin; wilfully lying in this as greatly as in the doctrine of the trinity of persons constituting one God; falsifying Scripture utterly.

CHAPTER V.

Heaven and Hell.

THE whole of the starry skies in the sight of God are as a little speck, a very minute ball, the sun being in the middle thereof; the very minute ball being surrounded by the illimitable heavens, the dwelling-place of God, of His glorious son, and of His holy angels—

the heavens, illimitable in extent, pervading all space outside the minute ball.

The greatest of all prizes is our entrance into heaven, to live there for ever with the Almighty God our loving Father, and with the loving, gentle, King Christ, our kind deliverer, and with the loving holy angels; and to be ourselves like them, loving and holy angels for ever. God has not given to man intelligence enough to conceive the glorious happiness in store there for the pardoned of mankind.

On the other hand, oh, ye nations! the greatest of all punishments, greater than the mind of man can possibly conceive, is for an immortal, disembodied soul to be shut out of heaven for ever, to be blotted out from the remembrance of God for ever, as mortified flesh that has been cut off to save a precious life. God will shield for ever his precious ones in heaven from their defiling presence; the dishonoured immortal souls of mankind are confined, as though they were dead, in one minute spot, small as the seed that was in Adam, in the *centre* of this round earth, which is called in Scripture the bottomless pit, for everywhere beyond the confined mass of dishonoured, condensed souls, there is an infinity of space. First, beyond it are the other parts of the earth, then beyond the earth are the starry skies, then beyond the starry skies is the infinite space of heaven.

This round earth is the only ball in all the vast infinity of space that is defiled with disobedience towards God.

The Almighty God foresaw, before beginning the creation of the starry skies, that many of the seed of Adam, during many of the first generations, would become vile and unworthy to enter heaven; but, again, he foresaw that in the later generations the seed in those vile men would become acceptable, pardoned children of God, in numbers innumerable as the sands upon the sea-shore; therefore God made man, giving him an immortal soul, and found a ransom for many. Alas, alas! that Adam fell! Alas, alas! for all who fall!

CHAPTER VI

Prayer.

MAN cannot imagine the shape of the Glorious Person of God, just as no person can imagine the shape of light. The invisible soul is after His likeness, but the visible body of man is not like God; and who can see the soul of man? Therefore, when we pray to God, not being able to see Him nor knowing His shape, we direct the attention of our souls towards heaven, far, far beyond the most distant star, and see by faith the glorious light that emanates from the Holy Person of God; but we do not see by faith God Himself, but only the glorious light—we cannot rightly imagine the shape of God.

The Holy Spirit of God alone can hear our prayer, for there is no other but the *one* God. The prayers of the God-fearing are telegraphed, as it were, to heaven by the Holy Spirit of God to the Glorious Person of God upon His throne, and to Christ upon the throne of His Kingdom; like as when our feet are touched, the touch is instantly telegraphed throughout the body.

When you have prayed that God may do a certain thing, sit not down idly, and foolishly imagine that God will do it without your further effort. The mere idle desire of man to obtain food is not sufficient to procure it, but the earth is ready to assist the efforts of man in obtaining it. Strive to do what you pray for, and, if your prayer be a wise one, the Holy Word of God will assist you wondrously; according to the strength and wisdom of your efforts, so will be your success. God makes *yourself* His instrument in carrying out your desire. God must see yourself in earnest, then His Holy Spirit will work with you in proportion as you are in earnest and spiritually wise.

In praying, we talk to the unseen Holy Spirit of God, who is ever near us; like as we talk in the dark to a loving friend, whom we know is close by, yet unseen; beseeching Him to forgive us our sins, fervently thanking Him for His inestimable love in finding a Mediator for us, and for His goodness in constantly controlling the sun, the moon, the countless stars, and this round earth, thereby ensuring our safety while upon earth, and our daily food. Beseeching Him not to shrink from us, but to make in us a dwelling-place of His Holy Spirit, that we may be in Him and He in us, and so be His holy children for ever, asking for these, and all the other holy desires of our souls, in the name of our Mediator, Jesus Christ, His Son.

Prayers uttered by the lips, aloud or silently, or silently by the soul, if with sincere fervour (for God loves not lukewarmness), are telegraphed to heaven by the Holy Spirit of God; but if insincere, or mere lip prayer, or uttered purposely before images or pictures, are not communicated to heaven, for they are as the evil words of the wicked, and as the bark of a dog, or the howl of a wolf, unworthy to be telegraphed to heaven.

Prayers for the dead are of no avail, for ever since the ascension of Christ, the great judge, immediately after death comes judgment.

The worship of God by prayer, by praise, and thanksgiving, God has declared to be man's holiest act, particularly if accompanied by acts of love and kindness towards mankind; for love of God begets a desire for the spiritual unity of all mankind, and begets softness of heart, especially towards those who love God, and begets pity towards those who are blinded by ignorance, and creates a strong, fervent desire that they also may become fellow worshippers—not a mere slothful wish, but an active desire to be of service in the holy cause, stirring the heart to deeds

The proper attitude in the sanctuary, and secretly in the closed room, while praying, is kneeling—the soul supplicating, and the body humbled.

Mankind worship God when their love of God prompts them to restrain their brutish passions and their brutish thoughts. Their good words and their good thoughts honour God, and so do their good deeds, for they are evidences of their faith in God; they honour God in that they proceed from creatures made by Him. But evil men are a dishonour to God, for they are His failures, therefore God does not love those who dishonour him.

When we pray with sincerity, God pardons all our past sins infinitely more freely than a loving mother pardons her loving child, and we are then perfectly sinless in His sight. But frequent prayer is needed, for we sin frequently, in sins of omission and commission, therefore we need frequently to be freed from them.

The influence of the weak in faith is weak indeed, but the influence of the strong in faith is strong indeed in behalf of a worshipper, but valueless in behalf of those who have no faith. It is honourable in the sight of God to pray for the wicked, but still more honourable to pray for those who possess faith. The prayers of all the world will not save the soul of a wicked man, but if that man repents him of his wickedness, and believes in God, and in Christ his Redeemer, supplicating for forgiveness through the great atonement, then God will pardon him, not because of the prayers of the world, but for his own prayers.

Recollect, my brother, and you, my sister, that God desires our chief aim to be, to live for ever in heaven. Beseech God only what you strive for: strive to obey Him in all things, and pray that all mankind may be led, through His Holy Word, to obey Him. Beseech Him to pardon your many sins and your many shortcomings, and the many sins and the many shortcomings of your fellows. Strive to understand His holy precepts, and beseech Him to give you a right understanding; and beseech Him to give all mankind a right understanding also. Strive to love all who love and reverence Him, and beseech Him to increase your love, and beseech Him to infuse His love in the heart of everyone; strive to spread around you a right knowledge of God, and beseech Him to assist you in your efforts; strive to alleviate the distresses of your fellows, and beseech Him to assist you; strive for unity in the Church of Christ, and beseech God to infuse unity of spirit among mankind; strive to be tender-hearted, and beseech God that all mankind may also be tender-hearted one towards the other; strive that all you do, all you say, all you think, and all you write, shall be in accordance with His holy desire, and beseech Him that all mankind, in all they do, in all they say, in all they think, and in all they write, may also be in accordance with His Holy Word. Be zealous in extending the Kingdom of Christ upon earth, and beseech God to infuse zeal into the hearts of His children. Strive to be as a stone to all temptation; to do, or say, or think, or write naught that is evil. Beseech Him to assist all mankind to overcome their evil passions, and all temptation; and finally, beseech Him that when you die, and as mankind die, all may be found acceptable heirs of the kingdom of heaven. Beseech for all these good things in the name and through the mediation of His Glorious Son our Saviour, the Messiah Jesus Christ, and God will esteem you holy and acceptable always.

Lift up your united voices aloud in praise and thanksgiving, in songs of sweet melody to God and His glorious Son; thanking God for having created you, for giving you a soul whereby you may worship Him; for His goodness in creating the beautiful earth for the sustenance of all His creatures; for the pleasant sunlight and the beauteous skies; for the glorious kingdom which He has prepared in heaven for His pardoned children; for giving us His written Word; for devising His glorious plan of redemption; for selecting the glorious Messiah whom He foreknew would succeed in ransoming us; for His great goodness in accepting the Messiah's great atonement as our atonement, as a dreadful debt paid in full; and for the infinite goodness of God in adopting us through that atonement as His children.

Furthermore, let us lift up our united voices aloud in praise and thanksgiving to our Holy Messiah for consenting, of his own free will, to leave for awhile the glorious joyous heaven to become a man like unto us, that he might by his perfect obedience to God in all things restore us to the favour of God, which mankind, through the disobedience of Adam, had lost. And let us lift up our united voices aloud in praises and thanksgiving to the glorious Messiah, for undergoing his many sufferings upon earth at the hands of our fellow men. For his perseverance while his soul was anguished by the wickedness and wilful blindness of men, and for undergoing during three days the dreadful penalty of bearing all the sins of mankind, whereby his body was unholy—every day, to one whose spirit was so holy, as a thousand years—on our behalf. Let us raise aloud in praise and thanksgiving, with sweetest music, to God and our Messiah, the heartiest songs, that our hearts may thrill with tenderness towards every creature upon earth.

Lift up your voices aloud in songs of melody, recalling to the memory one of the other the many mercies of our God, how that He spared our fathers, though their iniquity was as the iniquity of other men—and our iniquity before we rightly understood God even greater than theirs ; recall to the memory one of the other, in songs of sweet melody, the wondrous love of our God, and of His glorious conquering Son for us. And in songs of sweet melody let us cheer each other while journeying onward to our happy heavenly home; and bid each other wait patiently and hopefully for the opening of the gates of eternal life. No longer sad as each in turn enters there, but joyous that they have entered.

With hymns of praise, of joy, and thanksgiving, let the streets, and country roads, and fields, and woods, and rocks resound, as your processions thread the way on the sacred day of rest, in unison with all sorts of sweetest music, on every sunny day of rest and days of festival. For when the spirit of our Messiah actuates the nations of the world, then will the days of sadness be past, and joyousness pervade all people, no longer shy to mention aloud the name of God ; but all will rejoice to sing aloud towards heaven, uttering forth their happiness, and their beauteous sanctuaries shall be to them a place of spiritual comfort, and they shall be joyous in placing upon the altar there the gifts of loving hearts. And weariness of spirit shall be as a thing of the past, for their thoughts shall love to dwell upon the wondrous doings of God and upon the precious blood which bought us. And the heaping up of silver and gold and possessions shall no longer be our great aim ; and excessive labour shall be as a thing of the past. No longer will men be luxurious, but content ; and peace and good will pervade the hearts of all mankind. No longer will the spiritual teachers of the people strive one against the other, nor will the people; but to sweet music they will sing together in unison, for a right knowledge of the Word of God will bind them together in unity of soul, in bonds of peace and of mutual love. Their chanting voices will be heard in heaven, and the angels join in unison;

and from the one Church of Christ, diffused throughout the earth, will ascend to heaven continuously, now from one branch then from another, the sweet sounds of holy melody and holy prayer.

CHAPTER VII.

Justification by Faith.

WORSHIP is speaking reverently to the unseen God, believing Him to be near by, listening. Through the sacrificial death of the body of Christ, God has promised to pardon, and accept as his children, all who worship Him, having faith—the faithful until death.

Faith is thorough confidence in the Holy Scriptures, combined with sincere worship, so that having faith, the faithful become spiritually wise, united, holy, and joyous—joyous as a little child nestling in the bosom of his father, whom he fondly loves, and by whom he knows he is beloved. Like as the telescopes of man reveal countless stars, that are unseen to the unassisted eye, and like as the microscope reveals countless very minute living creatures, that are unseen to the unassisted eye, so faith reveals to him who possesses faith his own utter unworthiness, thereby leading him penitently to present to God the great atonement of Christ as his atonement; and it reveals to him the glorious power, might, majesty, and love of God, and His glorious presence, in us, around us, and everywhere.

Some of the wicked slightly believe in the existence of God. Nay, more, some of the wicked also slightly believe in the Scriptures being the revealed work of God. Nay, still more, they also slightly worship God. But these have not faith in the sight of God, for they believe a little, but disbelieve much ; they are obedient a little, but are disobedient much more ; they honor God a little by their worship, but dishonor Him still more by their folly ; they are men whose souls are in a mist, seeing a very little, spiritually, but their souls are withheld from seeing far, because of the mist of ignorance ; like as the lesser creatures are blinded by the mist of ignorance, so are they.

The greatest of all the works of man, in the sight of God, is faith, all other works in comparison are as dross. It is through faith the souls of mankind are saved. He who possesses faith will strive to add other good works thereto, according to the greatness of his faith ; will strive to do the will of God in all things, so as to become an obedient child of God ; will habituate himself to good thoughts and good deeds ; will love that which is good and abhor that which is evil ; will strive to spread widely His Holy Scriptures, and will strive to give mankind a right understanding of God, so that they may be of one mind in spiritual things.

No irreligious man, however extensive his good works, can be saved by them, for he is simply as a kind, harmless dove, or four-footed sheep, tender-hearted to his own kind, but rebellious towards God his Creator ; neither dove, nor sheep, nor faithless man will enter heaven, for he lacks the chiefest of all good works —the one thing needful—Faith. By faith, therefore, and through faith only, do men become holy in the sight of God, the holiness of Christ being thereby imputed to them.

CHAPTER VIII.

Confessing Sins.

THE Almighty God our Creator, and His Glorious Son our Messiah, alone can pardon the sins of any man. The pardon of God to a man ensues through the prayer for pardon of that man alone; therefore no other man can influence God in pardoning him. Were all the ministers of spiritual things, and all the rest of mankind, to pray with that man, and for that man, God pardons that man neither because of the prayers of the ministers, nor because of the prayers of the rest of mankind, but solely because of the prayer of the man himself. Believe not the lying ministers of spurious churches, who say, " Confess your sins to us, and *we* will pray to God, and He will pardon you;" but spurn ye the lying priests from your nation, for they lie, and wear the mask of holiness to glorify themselves in the estimation of the people. God hears not their prayers, for they are abhorrent to him, being liars. When you have sinned against any of mankind, confess your sin repentantly to that one, and strive to repair the injury ; then, after having striven, pray to God for forgiveness, and God will pardon you. Trust not to the prayers of others, but trust solely in your own prayer, for none but yourself can influence God and His Glorious Son in your behalf.

CHAPTER IX.

THE ORDINANCE OF BAPTISM.

LIKE as the holy ordinance of circumcision among the Israelites gave to the circumcised infants membership in the Jewish Church, whereby they were publicly acknowledged to be children of Abraham, so, under the dispensation of Christ, infants and converts are, in accordance with the holy ordinance of baptism, baptized by sprinkling them with water; thereby giving them membership in the one Church of Christ, whereby they are publicly acknowledged to be fellow-members, and all the members of the Church, through their ministers, solemnly bind themselves to teach and train aright all thus baptized. The rite of baptism by the sprinkling of water is a necessary Christian rite, in like manner as circumcision was a necessary Jewish rite; it confers holiness, inasmuch as it is an act of obedience to Christ—all acts done *purposely*, in obedience to the teachings of Scripture, are holy, and confer holiness on the doers: the water itself confers no holiness. Take tender care of the little children, for they are your successors, and joyously receive them as fellow-members.

This is the visible baptism by water.

There is another baptism, the *spiritual*, invisible baptism of the Holy Spirit of God, the living, invisible cloud, which thus takes place. When an infant, in process of time, understands the Gospel, and, believing in the mediatory death of Christ, worships God, supplicating for forgiveness of sins through that mediatory death, God pardons the sins of that soul, and the Holy Spirit of God joyously and lovingly enters into him, claiming him as a child of God. This is the inward baptism of the Holy Spirit, called the baptism through the blood or death of Jesus, because the Holy Spirit enters only into those who believe in the mediatory death of Jesus; it being only through his great atonement that mankind enter into heaven. So that it is necessary that each one of us should be baptized, not with water only, but with the Holy Spirit of God also.

It is good that the children of Christians should be baptized with water during their early infancy, for then, during their childhood, God graciously imputes to them the piety of their parents.

CHAPTER X.

The Ordinance of the Sabbath.

GOD has ordained that every seventh day should be a day of rest from servile work, both for man and for the cattle in the service of man, that the rich man, the poor man, the household servant, and the cattle, may enjoy a day of peaceful rest and serenity, and may all be equally free from toil on that day. Man may not do anything for hire, or buy or sell anything on that day; whatever be done, one to the other, must be done from kindness, and not for reward, for the Sabbath is the birthright of all mankind, and of the cattle in the service of man. Let no man defraud them of this their birthright; it is a treasure highly to be valued by all. He who labours voluntarily for hire on that day, when he might with safety rest, is a slave to his avarice and void of understanding, not comprehending the goodness and love of God for us in ordaining rest from servile work on the Sabbath day—a rest and change so necessary to all.

God has also commanded that the Sabbath should be kept holy, holy to the Lord, by fervently worshipping in the sanctuary on that day—not necessarily during the whole day, for that would be wearisome, lifeless worship, but part thereof. The day is to be made holy by the fervent worship of God in His sanctuary, this public worship making that day holy to the sincere and penitent worshipper, worshipping Him by also striving to restrain our inclinations to do or think evil, and in striving to help our fellow-kind in all good works.

Mere abstinence from servile work on the Sabbath day, without fervent public worship, does not make it holy.

To the God-fearing worshipper, after worshipping in the sanctuary, all things are holy on the Sabbath day. In toiling to relieve his fellow men from misery or pain; in toiling to spread a knowledge of God's will to the young, the middle-aged, and to the old; these things he may do, as a child of God, having spiritual love, for it is lawful to do any good thing on the Sabbath day. If a servant, she may perform acts of necessity, having spiritual love, but not for money. Take heed, ye nations! let not the servant be defrauded of the Sabbath day. Man may eat and drink moderately, and gently recreate. Eschew the acquisition of knowledge that relates to the handiwork of man, on the Sabbath day, but rather trace out the wondrous works of God, and strive to comprehend His Holy Scriptures.

The Sabbath is a day not of sadness but of holy joy, a day of rest from the cares and anxieties of our earthly life; a day of holy joy—joy to the soul and to the body, that the Lord our God has pardoned our sins in the midst of the congregation of His children, that we have been reconciled to Him there once more through the great atonement of our Messiah.

The godless are miserable, discontented, selfish, vicious,

cruel, morose, and downcast, because they know not God; but ye, worshippers of the Most High God, be ye joyous, because ye are His adopted children whom ye will soon see in that joyous heavenly house which has been prepared for all who love Him and His Glorious Son, our Messiah. Be ye therefore joyous, with a quiet, holy joy. And be stirring; show thy love to thy brethren, to those who are thy fellow worshippers, and to those who know not God. Let thy love win their hearts, that they may be desirous of being joyous and loving as thyself. Keep not thyself from thy fellow-kind, but mix with them, setting them a good example with humility. Draw them also to do well, especially the young; mould them to thy ways, but conform not in the least to their evil ways. Be watchful, therefore, over thyself, remembering that the Sabbath does not make thee holy, but thou, if thou art a sincere worshipper of God in His sanctuary, makest it holy to thyself. If thou art sick, and confined to thine house, thou makest it holy to thyself by privately worshipping God there. And when ye go among a nation of Sabbath-breakers, observe thou thy Sabbath, that they may understand how much more reasonable thy Sabbath is than theirs.

CHAPTER XI.

Ordinances.

THE ordinances of man, concerning spiritual things, are by themselves nothing; nay, the ordinances of God are by themselves nothing; nay, yet more, the Holy Scriptures, the Word of God, by themselves are nothing; they cannot by themselves alone, according to the law of God, save the soul of any man. For if a man were scrupulously to follow all the ordinances of God, and had in his memory every word in the Holy Scriptures, yet worshipped not God, his soul would not be saved, for he would still be unholy in the sight of God, a follower of mere outward ceremonials, a man not having the love of God in his heart. Therefore, ordinances by themselves are nothing; they are as roads leading to a great city, but are not the city itself. To the Israelites, the ordinance of circumcision and the ordinance of the passover were but aids to salvation, but were not salvation itself. In like manner, the ordinance of baptism, and the ordinance of the Feast of Unity (the Lord's Supper), are but aids. Ordinances are aids to unity, to mutual love, to separation of the faithful from the unfaithful, and for the partial separation of those of weak faith from those of strong faith.

CHAPTER XII.

Repentance.

REPENTANCE is belief in the existence of God, and of having misbehaved ourselves in word, thought, and deed in His sight, and of our utter unworthiness to enter heaven, where God is, without his pardon, sorrowing for past misdeeds, and humbly supplicating the pardon of God, through the mediatory death of Christ, the Messiah. Thus sincerely repenting, and sincerely supplicating God, He graciously pardons the penitent, His Holy Spirit no longer shrinks from him, but, being purified by pardon, His Holy Spirit lovingly and joyously enters into him, and claims him as an adopted child of God, and an inheritor of the kingdom of heaven.

Like as water washes the skin from filth, so the pardon of God purifies the soul from all past sins. The pardon of God is obtained first by believing in the mediatory death of Christ the Messiah, then by sincere repentance, then by sincere supplication to God for pardon, then by a sincere determination to strive to the uttermost against our evil thoughts, our evil words, and our evil deeds.

CHAPTER XIII.

Being Born a Second Time.

EVERY child when born is a descendant of disobedient Adam—Adam's child; but when he worships God aright, sincerely supplicating for forgiveness of sins, God pardons him, and His Holy Spirit enters into him, and claims him as a child of God, an inheritor of the kingdom of heaven; no longer a child of the man Adam, but the adopted child of God. This is the second birth.

CHAPTER XIV.

Election.

BEFORE God created the sun, the moon, the countless stars, and this round earth, He ordained that every one of mankind who received the baptism of His Holy Spirit, continuing faithful until death, should be elected to have heaven as his dwelling-place. Every man, every woman, and every child can receive the baptism of His Holy Spirit, the Holy

Spirit entering into them, God in them and they in God, by their believing and worshipping God, and striving to obey His Holy Scriptures. The obedient are the elect of God. He has elected, that is, chosen them as His children. With themselves alone it rests whether they obey or disobey, for God turns no man to the right hand nor to the left, neither to do a good thing nor to do an evil thing, only through His Holy Scriptures does God influence the heart of any man. Therefore, ye people, be not blind and superstitious in this matter; heaven is open to all who strive to obey God.

CHAPTER XV.

IDOLATRY.

THUS saith the Lord God, "Ye shall make ye no idols nor graven image, nor rear ye up a standing image, neither shall ye set up *any* image in your land to bow down before it, for I am the Lord your God."

No man hath seen God at any time; neither can any man have the least knowledge of the shape of God. Like as no man has the least knowledge of the shape of sunlight, or of the shape of the soul of man, therefore the wretched efforts of puny foolish man to represent God as of this shape or that shape, is dishonouring to God; and more dishonouring still that man, to whom He has given a soul, should become as unintelligent as a dog, by worshipping them; and behave as though he were mocking the unseen God, the Creator of all things.

And remember, oh ye nations, the mediatory death of Christ is to be held in remembrance; not by means of an image upon a cross, but like as we have God in our thoughts, or like as we have a distant relative in our hearts. What wouldst thou think of the man who could not remember his mother unless he had a plaster, or wood, or stone image, representing her? If thou, with thy limited wisdom, shouldst consider the man a fool, how much greater must his folly appear to the all-wise, all-powerful God, in the man supposing that a vile, inanimate image should be at all like God.

CHAPTER XVI.

The Beauty of Holiness.

BEHOLD, oh man, the countless stars, in number as the grains of sand upon the sea shore, innumerable. These, the sun, the moon, this round earth and all its contents, animate and inanimate, were made for man—for his pleasure and for his enjoyment—nevertheless, all these things in the sight of God are as dross compared to one holy angel; for those God can make at any time, and in any number; but one obedient angel, one tried angel, exceeds them all in value in the sight of God.

He has made countless living creatures for the benefit of man, but in His sight they are as grains of sand, because they worship not God more than do grains of sand. A worshipping man understands somewhat of God, therefore God accepts him as His child; but those who do not worship Him are of less value in His sight than grains of sand; for those who do not worship Him, being disobedient, are unholy, whereas grains of sand are not unholy.

The wicked man deceives himself, for his body is not more wonderfully made than that of other living creatures; therefore, thus far, they are equal, one not more highly prized than another. But a worshipping man exercises his soul and talks to God, speaking to Him as his Holy Father; and the Holy Spirit of God lovingly responds thereto, graciously enters into him, and claims him as His child; therefore His child is beloved, but the wicked man is despised.

Oh man! thou lovest thy dutiful son, thy loving son, wouldst thou part with him in exchange for thousands of lice, nay for millions of lice, nay for hundreds of millions of lice? You say "No!" in abhorence. Why not? for each one is a living creature, and as wonderfully made as the flesh and blood of thy son; nevertheless, thou hatest them but lovest thy son, for he is thy beloved child, whereas they are hateful vermin in thine eyes. In like manner, God considers each one of His children of more value than millions of wicked men, for He loves tenderly the one, but abhors intensely those millions. Abhorring them, but not the lice, for these cannot possibly comprehend God, but to wicked man God has given that power, and with it they worship Him not, but use their higher intelligence in mocking and despising Him.

As one sound seed that germs and becomes a goodly tree, exceeds in value all the seed which have rotted in the ground, not becoming trees, so does one worshipper of God in His sight exceed in value all the wicked men who have died in their sins, for they are His failures. In like manner as an husbandman sows many seeds, knowing that many of those he sows will never produce fruit, so God has sown the world with mankind, only a small proportion of whom have had the wit to understand that God, their Creator, is to be worshipped, and be supplicated for pardon through the mediatory death of Christ, and being pardoned, and converted to God, thereby yield unto God the good fruit of holiness. But hereafter the earth will become more fruitful in holiness, because the intelligence of mankind will be clearer, and then great will be the spiritual harvest of our God and of our Messiah. In like manner as God waited about 4000 years before He, through the Messiah, redeemed the soul of man, so God has waited for the great spiritual harvest the future will produce.

CHAPTER XVII.

Teachers of Spiritual Things.

GOD appoints neither the priests of the worshippers of the sun, nor the priests of the worshippers of the monkey, nor the man-eating priests of man-eaters, nor the priests of the worshippers of the crocodile, nor the priests of the worshippers of the serpent, nor the priests of the worshippers of Mary, nor the priests of the worshippers of Mahomet, nor the priests of the worshippers of other follies—no! nor even the ministers of the true worshippers of Himself!

God and the Messiah have commanded that mankind should select as their ministers holy men, and should utterly abhor and displace their spiritual teachers if unholy. In like manner as God has left to the free will of mankind to obey His holy precepts or to disobey, so He has given them free will to appoint, as their spiritual teachers, whom they may select; the Scriptures alone God has given as their guide to distinguish holy teachers from the unholy. He who teaches in accordance with the Scriptures is a worthy teacher, but he who teaches not in accordance is an impostor, abhorrent to God.

No one man has more power, spiritually, than another; all are equally powerless since the days of the last of the apostles; therefore if any man pretends to supernatural power, he is a liar. Holy men are not pretenders, it is the vile only who wish to deceive.

In the sight of God there is no occupation so honourable to mankind as that of a true spiritual teacher; and in the sight of man it should be the most honourable, also.

CHAPTER XVIII.

Ceremonials.

WHEN people congregate together for public worship, in prayer, in praise, and in thanksgiving, there must of necessity be order in their worship; therefore it must be ceremonious, otherwise it would be a confusion of tongues; for to worship publicly is to speak or sing to God *aloud* in unison, glorying that we have faith in God, not being ashamed to acknowledge Him *aloud* before our fellows—so that all public worship must of necessity be ceremonious. Now the lukewarm and the young are soon wearied by a long, monotonous ceremonial; their strength flags, and their ears become dull, and their understanding very weak, therefore they take no pleasure in their worship, it becomes a mere pretence, a mere sham, and, being tempted by the world, yield to its allurements. Therefore the ceremonial must not be monotonous, but varied, and stirring; stirring with songs of praise, songs of thanksgiving, and with songs cheering one another in their journey towards heaven, with sweet music to aid and lead the people.

In the ceremonial by itself, or in the music by itself, there is no efficacy; the honour done to God is in the holy utterances which proceed from the stirred hearts of the sincere worshippers. Ceremonials and music are simply aids to the people, to neutralize their tendency to weariness, and to sing and pray in unison.

CHAPTER XIX.

The Sanctuary.

THE Sanctuary is a building consecrated to the use of the God-fearing, wherein they may assemble together, and unitedly worship God aloud. The building simply shields them from the weather, shielding them from the rain, the sun, and wind; liable to be destroyed by lightning, by wind, by fire, by earthquake, and by time. It is called the House of God, because it is set aside wholly for the use of the worshippers of God, wherein they may publicly acknowledge God in the presence of mankind. The bricks, the stone, the mortar, and the wood, used in the building thereof, and its decorations, are not esteemed in the sight of God, the creator of the starry skies; but His Holy Spirit enters largely into the penitent while congregated there; their hearts are the living temples of the Most High God. The bricks, the stone, the wood, and the mortar, are as dross in His sight; but the soul of even one penitent is as a pearl of great price, and the congregation of many penitents is greatly esteemed by the Most High God. Nevertheless, the building being set aside for holy purposes, is not to be lightly esteemed, nor too highly regarded—not superstitiously. Its value, in the sight of God, consists in its being the place where His children upon earth meet unitedly to worship Him; without them it is as dross in His sight, but with them it is a holy house; therefore no one part of the building is holier than another.

There is no need for a sacrificial altar in the sanctuary. A sacrificial altar was truly needed under the Mosaic dispensation, because then the blood of slain creatures was shed upon it as a sacrifice unto God, that by this act of obedience to God the Israelitish worshippers might have removed from them temporarily, until the mediatory death of the Messiah, the curse wherewith God cursed Adam. But the sacrificial death of Christ, which took place not upon an altar, nor was his body placed upon an altar, but upon a vile instrument of murderers, was an all-sufficient atonement once and for ever for the removal of the curse wherewith God cursed Adam from every one of Adam's descendants; therefore, no more sacrifice of blood is needed, consequently no sacrificial altar is needed. The only sacrifice man now offers is a penitent, worshipping soul, which cannot be placed upon an altar of brick, or stone, or wood, for it is enshrined in the living altar of his body; therefore, the presence of a sacrificial altar in a sanctuary is a sign that the worshippers there do not rightly understand the dispensation of Christ. Where several followers of Christ assemble to worship God, there especially is the spirit of belief in the Messiahship of Christ among them, leading them to unite in prayer and in songs of praise, acknowledging him *aloud* as their Messiah.

CHAPTER XX.

God is the only Invisible Spirit near to Man.

THE wickedness that exists among mankind, God has mercifully shielded from the angels in Heaven—they can neither see us, nor we them—they live in the joyous heavens, with God and His Glorious Son; never visiting the earth—neither has the Glorious Messiah visited the earth since his ascension. The pardoned souls of the righteous, are at their death, at once carried lovingly into heaven—the souls of the unpardoned wicked ones are, at their death, at once sent into perdition, far away for ever from mankind. The Holy Spirit of God alone is the only invisible spirit that is ever near to man—

therefore, ye nations, be neither foolish nor superstitious; nor permit at any time superstitious notions to be mentioned, for they are antagonistic to a right understanding of the Holy Scriptures.

CHAPTER XXI.

The Providence of God.

THE Almighty God has framed certain laws for His own guidance in governing the things in heaven, in the starry skies, and in the earth—laws that are unchangeable.

The angels in heaven have perfect free will, and being exceedingly wise, righteous, and filled with the Holy Spirit of God, are holy always, obeying the precepts of God for their guidance in all things.

The orbs in the starry skies being inanimate, obey perfectly the laws of God—the inanimate things of the earth being inanimate, also obey perfectly the laws of God; so that summer and autumn, winter and spring, day and night of varying lengths, clouds and sunshine, the ground and the waters producing food for the support of living things, ensue generation after generation.

Living things of the earth, in many things obey the laws of God intuitively—in other things they neither obey nor disobey, in that God has not given them the intelligence to understand His Holy Scriptures. To man alone, God has given the tremendous power of disobeying Him, by giving him a soul, that holy thing capable of comprehending the precepts of God— and giving to that soul free will.

God gave to man a soul and free will, that by comprehending and obeying God of his own free will, not being coerced by Him— of man's own free will, obeying God, as do the holy angels— man might live for ever in heaven as the angels. Without a soul and free will, man would have been as the lesser creatures, the cat, the dog, and the like, utterly unable to commune with God, therefore, like them, utterly unworthy to enter heaven, and utterly unworthy to be the companions and equals of the holy intelligent angels of God.

To naught out of heaven, except to mankind, has God given a soul and free will—gifts of inestimable value to all who use them aright, in that through them they become angels in heaven; but gifts greatly to be dreaded by all who use them in disobeying the precepts of God, as revealed in the Holy Scriptures.

God shields mankind from every deviation of the stars, or earth, or sun, or moon ; causes the sun to shine, the clouds to give out their beneficent moisture, and the ground to give up its treasures, for He compels them to obey perfectly His laws. But God does not shield you, oh, unwise nations ! from the consequences of your ignorance of God, of your injustice, nor of your other follies, neither your people from the bitter consequences of their wickedness one towards the other. God has commanded and given you the power to shield yourselves from the wickedness one of the other, by your inculcating right knowledge and uprightness among all mankind. Obey God !

God has laid down the law that he will turn no man either to the right hand or to the left, neither to do a good thing nor to turn him from any evil thing, excepting only through His advice, as recorded in the Holy Scriptures, neither urging the elements nor holding them back; reserving to Himself to set that law aside temporarily for certain great purposes, as when God, on behalf of the prophets, worked miracles, and prompted them to prophecy, and to do and write certain things for the instruction of man, that man might comprehend the will of God.

CHAPTER XXII.

The Resurrection.

GOD formed Adam, giving him an invisible spirit and a visible body in *temporary* union, providing him with a body capable of perpetuating his own kind, and furnishing it with eyes of limited vision—eyes incapable of seeing God, or the holy habiters of heaven. When death is ensuing, all things become dim, and the things of earth and the starry skies seem to fall and melt away before the eyes, no more to be seen by those eyes for ever; the union of the body with the soul is severed, never again to be re-united. The invisible spirits of the children of God, no longer trammelled with flesh and blood, instantly see God and His Glorious Son, becoming angels without bodies, like to the other angels in heaven; but their bodies of flesh and blood left behind them upon the earth, as unworthy to enter heaven, become dissolved, never again to be their bodies, like as a candle, when burnt, is annihilated as a candle, dispersing, never again becoming a candle.

The dying infant rises not again as an infant, neither an old man as an old man, neither the decrepit as decrepit, neither a husband as a husband, nor a wife as a wife, neither a maid as a female, nor a young man as a male; their souls alone, which are neither male nor female, but like to the image of God, rise to immortal life in heaven, never again to be united with anything that shall die. In heaven there is neither marriage nor giving in marriage. The body God fashioned that it might perpetuate mankind over all the earth; being only fitted for the earth, it remains within the earth; being part of the earth, it continues as part of the earth. But the soul, not being formed out of the constituents of the earth, remains not within the earth, but is carried into heaven, its native home, excepting those condemned to be shut up in the bottomless pit for ever.

Before the Messiah rose from the dead, after his crucifixion, and ascended into heaven, all the souls of mankind that had been provisionally pardoned were asleep in Paradise, in a beauteous orb of the starry skies; and the souls of the wicked were also asleep in a part of the earth God had set apart for them, far away from all mankind. When the Messiah had ascended into heaven, the Almighty God, our Creator, placed His victorious Son on the throne of his kingdom, next in power to Himself, and appointed him King over all the redeemed souls of mankind, and the Great Judge and Intercessor of all mankind. Then quickly the souls of the good in Paradise were awakened, and tenderly, and lovingly carried by the Holy Spirit of God into heaven, and a large measure of His Holy Spirit there given to each soul, being pardoned through the mediatory death of Christ. The sleeping souls of the wicked were then awakened, and being judged by the Great King, the Christ, were condemned as unworthy to enter heaven; quickly their souls were driven into perdition, and there shut up from everything else for ever. Thereafter, as mankind died, they were instantly judged by the Great King, and rewarded or condemned. And those of us now alive, who have the *seal* of Christ upon us as God's children, will be caught up and carried into heaven instantly the soul separates from the body.

End of Part IV.

CHRIST IS COMING.

PART V

RE-ORGANIZATION OF THE ONE HOLY UNIVERSAL CHURCH OF CHRIST.

CHAPTER I.

To the Nations.

LOOK around you, oh ye nations! upon all the people throughout the world, and mark how much alike they are in doing evil, because of their ignorance in comprehending God. Verily, verily, they are very much more like brutes than like the angels in heaven; they have fallen greatly, so greatly, that they have become as mere intelligent cattle. Whose is the fault? The fault, the terrible fault, is that of the law-makers, the present and the past, who have been more intent upon enriching and raising themselves over their fellowmen than in instilling right knowledge into the people; they have been more intent in retaining their position as masters, and the people as servants ministering to their luxuries, than to raise the thoughts of themselves and people towards God, who is the Almighty Benefactor of all mankind alike. The law-makers mould the ways of the nation for good or evil; hitherto they have been evil, therefore the nations have been moulded into evil ways and evil thoughts. And now behold, ye nations! your law-makers are as the officers of a ship whose rudder has been shivered by the tempestuous waves, amid rocks on every side, one narrow channel only being open, through which the ship unwisely entered. Those officers shall be deposed, and the guidance of the ship back through the narrow channel and to a right course entrusted to wise hands, and they shall succeed.

The chiefest of all the duties of the law-makers of a nation, is to do their very utmost that in spiritual things the people be not deceived, for if the rulers permit them to be deceived by one society or by another, assuredly strife and disorder will reign in that nation so long as the people are being deceived, for certain of the most right-minded of the people will resist the spiritual deception, and will expose the deception in its nakedness. The law-makers of a nation are utterly unworthy to be law-makers if they neglect this, the chiefest of all their duties, for through their negligence they are not promoters of concord, but of discord; therefore as baneful as a pestilence among the people.

It is the fault of the law-makers that spiritual error is so rife among the nations, the law-makers have, as it were, given licence to clerics to deceive the people in spiritual things; therefore the people are very evil through being kept in ignorance of God. In temporal things the rulers strive through their laws to restrain fraud, but do not check spiritual fraud, which is greatly more mischievous than the other. The clerics require to be restrained, for they are but men, and all men are at times tempted by ambition, and some fall away; they should not be permitted to teach aught that is spiritually untrue. You inquire, What is truth? Truth is not a lie! Therefore, when a cleric teaches that himself or fellow clerics have greater spiritual power than other men in any one thing, and is unable to prove his assertion satisfactorily to the common sense of mankind, let the law-makers sternly prohibit him any longer from teaching the people, for being a liar he is utterly unworthy. It is the desire of lying clerics to cause the people to be superstitious, that they may be able the more effectually to defraud them, and to hold clerics in superstitious reverence. It is the law-makers who err, for they, being the rulers of the people, should shield them not only from the thief but from the clerical defrauder, who is greatly more mischievous than the thief, in that he causes the people to become superstitious and foolish, teaching them things that are untrue. When clerics become teachers of truth, the people will love them because they are teachers of truth, and worthy living examples to their fellow-men.

And ye professing Christians throughout the world, mark how different are the teachings of the many sects one from the other; every one teaches differently from the holy teachings of God. Not one truly comprehending even that foundation of all religion—the holy plan of God; therefore they necessarily miscomprehend His holy teachings. All travel their separate paths; all diverge more or less from the main road. Truly ye have much of the truth, but ye have much of error also; your errors mar greatly the truth that is in you.

There is hardly anything so foolish but that many of the thoughtless, the foolish, and the ignorant of a nation will not believe, if the spurious church of that nation does but teach it, for there is great weight in the eyes of the people in the church that is endowed by the nation; therefore it is very hard to weed from the endowed church of a nation any foolish doctrine. It is not well, oh ye law-makers! to permit any church society to be endowed by the state, nor permit any church society to be endowed with riches; what it yearly requires should be yearly earned. Cease to endow! be not afraid, for like as the goldsmith refines his gold, separating it from the dross, so will you separate spiritual gold from spiritual dross. Remember always that an endowed spurious church is a thorn to the right-minded, for it is a perpetuator of evil, a very brand of discord, a breeder of sects, and a prolific breeder of idle pretentious priests. On the other hand, the true church requires no endowment, for the true children of God love to be the stewards of Christ, their king.

The endowment of spurious churches is the cause of their perpetuation; being superstitious, lukewarm towards God, and nonsensical, they cannot stand without being endowed. Cease to endow! let not any of your religions be endowed, for endowment is the source and perpetuator of many evils; let them neither retain buildings nor land, except that retained for their religious purposes, nor suffer them to hoard; what they yearly require let them yearly earn from their own followers. Then will endowed lies, and endowed spiritual pretenders melt away, and one by one the many disunited sects will fall, but the followers of the true religion will grow in numbers and usefulness.

Now understand, oh, ye nations! if you desire to perpetuate discord, endow; but if you desire your people should live happily together, and prefer good to evil, then let not one of your religions be endowed. The followers of the church that is true will labour joyously for her needs, but the followers of a spurious church will unwillingly labour to uphold what is spurious, and little by little they will leave it to perish. Fear not! the evil, disuniting influence of the spurious sects will be shattered to pieces, and in its stead shall be unity and concord among mankind; evil things will decompose and afterwards become good things. Fear not, therefore, but boldly and promptly disendow every religion in your nation—it is enough for a state to teach the young, and hold fast the holy Scriptures purely. In proportion to your promptitude in these things, oh ye nations! so shall your misery be shortened.

Behold! the time is at hand when the spurious churches of the whole world will fall, because of their nonsense, and their unwise followers will be sorrowful; but when the beauteous, true old Church of Christ rises on their site, then will the hearts of all mankind rejoice; their sorrow will be but for a little while, but their joy God will perpetuate for ever.

And remember always, ye nations, that the children of God can govern their society better, far better than the temporal rulers can govern it. The meddling of temporal rulers is as a thorn to the true church, a very brand of discord, a great evil; therefore, ye nations, let the true church govern herself.

Understand clearly, oh ye nations of the whole world! the children of men are born into the world without knowledge, but they acquire knowledge as they grow, either good or bad, according to what they see and hear, righteously inclined if well nurtured and rightly taught, evil inclined if left in ignorance or wrongly taught. The welfare of a nation depends wholly upon the right or wrong spiritual training of the people. Were the people to be ever so skilful in things appertaining to things of the earth, they would be an evil people, rioting in wickedness, if they obeyed not God. On the other hand, were the people very unskilful in all earthly things, yet had love for God and for mankind in their hearts, they would be an estimable, holy people in the sight of God. Therefore, above all things, a wise nation should instil into the minds of all the children of that nation a knowledge of the Holy Scriptures; a wise nation should claim all the children born in the nation, and living within the boundaries of the nation, as in the guardianship of the nation. The nation shall not suffer anyone to stand in the way of a thorough knowledge of the Scriptures being grafted in the children of the nation; this shall be the sacred duty of the nations; they shall not heed the many sects. The Holy Scriptures shall be to a nation as its church —the Holy Scriptures as accepted by the present Trinitarian Church of England, for they are not adulterated. It shall be the sacred duty of every nation to educate all their children in a knowledge of the Holy Scriptures as they are, without straining them to suit this doctrine, or that doctrine, by trustworthy instructors approved of by the nation. Until the age of, at least, fourteen years, shall every child be educated; it shall be accounted an abominable thing, disgraceful to the nation, for a child not to be educated, in that every child has a sacred claim to be taught how to save his soul.

The children of a nation shall be deemed to be in the guardianship of the whole nation, entrusted by the nation to the subguardianship of their parents. Should the parents neglect their duty, then shall the education of the children be undertaken by the nation at some cost to the parents. No one shall be suffered to stand in the way of the education of the children of a nation. If a man be satisfied himself to be a fool, it shall not be suffered that he also make his children fools; if a man be mulish in this sacred thing, he is unworthy to have the charge of his children; it shall not be suffered that children should, by the neglect of anyone, breed evil in a nation. Ignorance of the Holy Scriptures, by the great mass of a nation, is the foundation of all the evils in a nation, whereas a right knowledge throughout the nation secures peace and happiness; therefore every nation shall consider it a sacred duty that every child be taught that *foundation* of all true knowledge, a knowledge of the Holy Scriptures. Then will the laws of every nation become just and equitable, the people happy, and true followers of Christ, worshipping God from the heart; then will all the nations be united together, each nation a separate branch of the one old Church of Christ.

CHAPTER II.

Spurious Churches.

LOOK around you, oh ye nations of the whole world, upon the many religions. Is there one that is sound, one that is based wholly upon the word of God, and governed in accordance with it? No, there is not one; each is unsound, from the crown of the head to the sole of the foot; each has gone astray, therefore they will fall, and greatly will mankind rejoice hereafter, that they have fallen never more to rise again.

Idolaters.

Listen thou Papacy—chief of idolaters; thou deceiver, calling thyself a Christian church, whereas thou art not so, thy idolatry severing thee from the Lord Christ; thou mystifier and perverter of the Holy Scriptures, to serve thy idolatrous practices; thou enemy of mankind; the destroyer of souls that place their trust in thee; the stumbling-block of the whole world, therefore the chief of the vile ones—know now that the God of Heaven has shut his ears from thee, He refuses to hear thy prayers always, because thy hypocritical priests have long perverted His holy teachings, that they might raise themselves above their fellows, and take the place of God, and of His Son;

teaching them the foolish doctrine of the trinity; to bow and utter prayers before images—God's abhorrence; teaching them to worship relics even, in thy great folly, spurious relics; teaching them to worship bread, and worship wine; to kneel before priests, confessing sins to those priests habitually; teaching the people that thy priests have power, supernatural power, to forgive sins, thereby in thy great arrogance falsely pretending that thy spurious priests are even holier than the holy angels of heaven, who never have sinned, for they possess not such great power. From thy very commencement thou hast been false, more ambitious to raise thy priests above other men than to obey God; more arrogant in thy pretentiousness, and more cruel towards thy fellow men, than ever were the godless. Thou hast been more prominent than other sects, because of thy stricter discipline, of thy greater audacity, of thy dissimulation, of thy great cunning, and because thou hast kept thy people from knowing aught in scriptural things other than what thy spurious priests teach them; so that thou hast compelled them through their ignorance to be of thy spurious church. Nevertheless, many despise thee, for clearly they see on thy frontlet, "Liar!" stamped deeply. They have become bewildered, reckless of the future, and unbelievers in God, because of thee, and thy people have become almost as senseless as the heathen. Now know, that from thy commencement the Holy Spirit of God has refused to communicate thy prayers to God in Heaven. As thou hast refused to pray to Him, as *all* the holy men of old prayed, purely without images, He also has refused to listen to thy impure supplications. Where has His word taught thee to use images? Where to worship bread, and worship wine? Where to reverence relics? Where has it taught thee, that the people should habitually confess their sins to any priest? Where has it taught any priest to be a pretender to supernatural power?

Where has it taught thee that any priest has power to pardon sins, or authority to receive the kneeling reverence of men? Where has it taught thee to arrogate thyself most presumptuously before God and man? The indictment is long, nevertheless it is not yet finished. Where has it taught thee that God is three separate persons? Where to pray to thy suppositious saints? Where has it taught thee to enjoin men to pray to imaginary saints, whom thou canonizest from time to time? Where has it taught thee to worship a Queen of Heaven? And where has it taught thee, thou adulterator of Scripture to suit thy follies and thy idolatry, that thy judgment is unerring, and that the judgment of the vilest of thy predecessors was unerring also? The Holy Scriptures nowhere tell thee these things. Thou pretendest to thy people that thy spurious church is founded upon the Holy Scriptures; thy doctrines and thy cruelty towards the readers of those Scriptures, who were in thy power, give thee the lie, for thou hatest the Scriptures, and greatly fear their spread among mankind, lest their eyes should be opened and thou shouldest be seen to be but a mere idolatrous, spurious church, whose doctrines are not the doctrines of Scripture. Thy spurious church is based upon lies, and not upon God's word, like to the spurious church of Mahomet; the name of Christ is to thee but a mask. Therefore God has shut His ears always, and has not heard thee, for thou art a spurious church. Yet a little while, and the earth shall know thy place no more for ever.

The Non-Idolatrous Sects.

Ye peoples who have separated yourselves from the great apostacy of Rome, ye did well in so doing; nevertheless, ye have not cast aside all her abominations, ye have prayed to God without images, therefore His Holy Spirit has heard thy prayers; but where has His Word taught thee that God was three separate persons? Where that the Lord Christ's feast was otherwise than a bond of spiritual love and union to the children of God, in remembrance of the great love of Christ for man, and of the great atonement? Where has it told thee that thy clerics have greater spiritual power than His children? Where has it taught thee that the ministers of thy many antagonistic sects were chosen by God to be thy spiritual teachers? Where does it teach thee that clerics are otherwise than simple leaders of His people, and teachers of His Holy Word? Where has it taught thee that thou mayest, without great sin, separate thyselves from the children of God, as though thou hadst no part nor lot with them, and as though thou refusest to put on the wedding garment of mutual love and unity of purpose? Nowhere has it told thee; thou hast greatly erred in not shaking thyself perfectly free from the great apostacy.

Is it in obedience, oh ye peoples, to the holy precepts of God, that you are split into so many discordant sects? Is it because ye think yourselves the children of God? Is it not rather because ye are children of selfishness, of deceit, of sensuality, of spiritual pride, of obstinacy, of spiritual ignorance, and children of disobedience towards God and His glorious Son? Is it not because ye are not truly the children of God? Deceive yourselves no longer, the children of God are not like you.

How comes it to pass, oh ye spiritual teachers, that your people listen to you in the sanctuaries, month after month, year after year, yet fail to comprehend God and His Messiah? Is it not because yourselves were bewildered by your predecessors, and in your turn ye bewilder and leave unconvinced your flocks; so that in spiritual things they are even greater blunderers than yourselves? Truly, both they and you greatly dishonour God, because of your nonsense. Ye unwise teachers, first lay the foundation of the Holy Scriptures firmly in your own minds, and in the minds of your flocks—the foundation being the mighty plan of God—then build your superstructure; ye have erred greatly in dwelling wholly upon the superstructure, neglecting the sure foundation; and ye have also greatly erred in not sufficiently striving for unity among yourselves.

Ye did well, ye peoples, in separating yourselves from the vile Papacy; and ye did well in separating yourselves from the corrupt lukewarm churches that came out of her; but ye all did evil in not uniting yourselves together, and ye did great evil in separating yourselves upon things of small doctrine—some of you even separating yourselves because you preferred one form of service in the sanctuary to another—esteeming very lightly the great doctrine of spiritual love and unity among all mankind, a doctrine of great estimation in the sight of God, the broad foundation of the one true Church of Christ. Deceive yourselves no longer, the angels of heaven know of no severance in spiritual things, one from the other, therefore you are not like them. Ye believe in God, the Almighty Creator of all things, in the great atonement of His glorious Son the Messiah, and in the truth of the Holy Scriptures, these three doctrines are the three great doctrines of the true Church of Christ, out of which proceeds the fourth great doctrine of spiritual love and unity among the children of God. If one of these four be wanting, then is the church not true, but spurious, like to those who supplicate before images or pictures. He neither heeds their impure supplications nor yours, for He abhors their images and pictures, and your wilful severance one from the other.

Ye deceive yourselves, ye many diverse sects; ye have

become superstitious as the Papacy, but differently; in many things nonsense has in your hearts usurped the place of common sense, therefore you widely differ one from the other in your interpretation of the Holy Scriptures. Ye are not wise. Ye account yourselves followers of Christ, but ye dishonour him, for you obey him like as the rabble soldiers of an undisciplined army obey their chief, obeying him a little in the lesser things, but disobeying him much in the greater ones. Ye err greatly in supposing that God selects your spiritual teachers to be your spiritual teachers; He neither turns them to the right hand nor to the left hand, nor you; neither is it God nor His Holy Scriptures that prompt you to hate each other, even to glory in your spiritual separation one from the other, but the brutish passions and spiritual ignorance of your spiritual teachers and of yourselves. Ye rival sects! you are as the brutish clans of a divided nation, not the source of strength to the kingdom of Christ upon earth, but the source of great weakness. Ye deem yourselves the children of God, but the true children of God are not undisciplined and disunited as are you. They neither eat alike nor drink alike, no, not even are they wise alike; but they love God alike, and His glorious Son our Redeemer, and all love the Holy Scriptures with real love, for to them it is not as a book that is sealed, and they have zealous love for each other and for all mankind. These are the signs of the true children of God, signs that are wanting in you, oh ye disunited peoples. Ye are as the camp followers of an army, disorderly, disintegrated, independent, captious, and not the true army of the Lord Christ; ye are but savage followers, hating each other, separating yourselves one from the other through imaginative nonsense; but for calling yourselves His followers, mankind would not know you were spiritual soldiers of the army of Christ, your ways are so much like the ways of the godless.

You deceive yourselves, oh ye sects, in permitting your ministers to pray in the stead of yourselves; henceforth pray for yourselves, sometimes aloud, like as you sing aloud, in unison. You do well in your singing aloud, do also well in your praying aloud. Ye go to the sanctuaries as listeners, ye should also go as talkers and singers to God and His glorious Son; as responding assentors to the prayers of the minister; and as listeners, communing with God and His glorious Son in talking and in singing; but most of you are as mutes, contentedly so. Ye deceive yourselves, oh ye sects, for your sincere prayers aloud, and your sincere songs aloud, are the main things in your religious services; the preaching of your spiritual teachers is of less account, intended principally for the idle and the ignorant. But the strong in faith need not the preaching, for themselves search the Scriptures, understanding them equally with the preacher.

The small things of the earth engross too much of your thoughts, and things of God too little; therefore your hearts towards God and towards mankind are very cold. Ye are not really children of God, but children of the world, for the children of God have not hearts of ice, but warm hearts of love for Him, for His glorious Son, and for all mankind. It is because of the frostiness of your hearts that ye keep yourselves apart from the children of God. Ye have been taught to dislike small spiritual things, and to have cold hearts, because of the icy hearts of your spiritual teachers. They, finding themselves in the ministry of a sect, have no wish to be convinced of their want of spiritual love, lest through following the dictates of conscience, their daily food and the daily comforts of their families should be lessened. Therefore they strive to keep you apart, not for your sakes, but for their own temporal things. It is they who teach you to keep apart, one from the other, and poor foolish weaklings, you take their will to be your will. Deceive yourselves no longer, your frosty hearts are not like the warm loving hearts of the children of God, whose hearts yearn and strive for spiritual unity.

Ye have become icy, oh ye sects! because ye have neglected congregating daily in the sanctuaries of your God. Ye have habituated yourselves by your severance one from the other to congregate together only on the Sabbath Day, therefore you have become cold-hearted, and your assembling on the Sabbath in the sanctuaries has become mere form. You do not assemble even on the Sabbath Day out of real warm love for God, but because it is more wearisome not to assemble than to assemble. Verily ye have frosty hearts. On the Sabbath Day ye appear to be followers of the Messiah—lukewarm followers only; but on every other day ye have no appearance of being his followers, for ye act as those who do not pretend to be his followers—in this ye are less than the sincere followers of the Papal sect—truly ye are not children of God! Your children's children will wonder and be sad because of your cold-heartedness, they will have greater love and be wiser than yourselves.

The Holy Spirit of God has been grieved that ye were so blind, ye have mystified yourselves about that which is plain, and therefore art split into many sects, and have become almost powerless in winning souls to Christ. Thy faith is very weak and bewildered; the enemies of God have their say against Him, and thou poor foolish weaklings, cannot answer them convincingly, and even are afraid of them; some of ye even partly coincide with their foolish utterances, so that the fools think they have gained the victory. Ye have left the main road, and every sect has strayed into bye-paths of folly; all are in error and shall understand they are so. Repentantly ye shall return to the main road of spiritual truth, with kindliness of heart and unity of purpose, and with real spiritual love ye shall hold out the hand of fellowship one to the other, and walk amicably together as become the true children of God, bewildering yourselves no more for ever.

Yet a little while, and the people having their spiritual eyes opened will leave all the sects of the whole world—all being the sects of Babel confusion and nonsense—in abhorrence of their cold-heartedness, their selfishness, their spiritual ignorance, and their wickedness, and will enter the true Church of Christ and be one with her for ever. You believe in God, in the Messiah, and in the divine inspiration of the Holy Scriptures; what hinders you from uniting yourselves to those who also zealously believe in them? what hinders you from being baptized into the only true Church of Christ, and be instrumental for great good, and not as heretofore, powerless excepting for evil? There is naught to hinder you excepting only your former habits, therefore with wise resolve be baptized at once, and happiness, which hitherto you have not known, shall alight and rest upon you always.

The Trinitarian Church of England.

What shall I specially say to thee, thou lukewarm church, thou church still retaining many errors thou hast imbibed from Rome; thou church of the rich and not of the poor, thou church neither hot nor cold, thou church of Babel disorder and clerical rebellion. Sitting quietly down while myriads of thy people are utterly ignorant of God; placidly regarding thyself when thou oughtest to humble thyself to the very dust for thy great negligence in not winning their souls to Christ. They hunger strongly for spiritual knowledge, and behold! the little bread of life thou offerest is so mixed with thy chilling and upstart pretentiousness, and so clothed with thy mysterious nonsense, that they cannot eat it, because it is loathing to their common sense. Thou offerest to many nothing, and to a few, as it were that stone, a thing indigestible to their souls. They ask of thee the pure Water of Life, and behold! thou offerest to them water made muddy by thy bewildering nonsense, so that they refuse to drink it: therefore myriads of the people of thy nation live and die as cattle, utterly ignorant of God. They are as abominable in the sight of God as were the heathen of old, because of thy negligence and self-complacency.

Thou hast complacently suffered the lay powers of the nation, who were oft times disbelievers and enemies of God, to control, gag, and play the fool with thee, as their price for endowing thee. They have held thee in check, and been thy master, so that thou hast ever been a make-believe church, a mill-stone about the neck of all that is good in the nation. Thou hast caused the children of God to become split into many sects through thy lukewarmness in the cause of God and thy superciliousness towards the people, that great sin lies at thy door. Some of thy clerics are now sighing to awaken thee, but thou art drowsy, and others of thy clerics are cunningly carrying thy people into the vile Papacy, imitating it in their temples, rearing images over sacrificial altars, and there fooling before them. Still thou art drowsy. The bribes the enemies of God, the disunited discordant law-makers of the nation, give thee in endowing thee and thy fatness, make thee drowsy, and thy connection with the lay powers of the State, makes thee powerless, for thou art an obedient servant, contentedly so, of unwise discordant men. Wherefore is it that thy comparatively few temples are almost deserted by the very numerous poor, and have become assemblies for display of clothing? Wherefore is it that thy higher clerics shamefully neglect their duty, receiving too much gold, becoming rich, luxurious, and cold-hearted towards God, and supercilious towards the poor; and thy lesser clerics discontented and unruly? Wherefore is it that thy lesser clerics are suffered to beard with impunity their congregations, and thy higher clerics are suffered to breed disunion, cold-heartedness, and hatred among them—the very opposite of the feast of unity? Wherefore is it that thou dost complacently, year after year, suffer clerics, perchance unworthy clerics, to be appointed over congregations by laymen, perchance members of the vile Papacy, others perchance even infidels and the vilest in the nation, and to buy and sell thy clerical appointments as though they were bartering for oil or wine? And wherefore is it that so many of thy clerics are so eager for promotion, not because of their zeal for the Messiah, but to satisfy their avarice, their love of ease, and their fondness for display? Wherefore is it that so many of thy clerics are ready to have their photographs displayed, but to feed their vanity, to the great scandal of the people? And wherefore sufferest thou some of thy clerics to retain each one of them several appointments, that they may become rich in gold?

The enemies of God mock Him; and thou, poor weakling, art as one dumb, having no plain convincing arguments to turn them from being the enemies of God into His worshippers. Go, give place! the Lord God and His Messiah disown thee; thou art in the way. Yet a little while, and thou shalt be dissolved utterly.

The Israelites.

And now, ye seed of Abraham, ye children of Israel, ye mourners, ye grief stricken, God's grief is as your grief, that

He has long listened but has not heard your suppliant cry. His Holy Spirit cannot, will not, transmit your prayers to God in Heaven, for ye despise the Holy One, His Son. Hitherto ye would not that the Messiah, Christ, should be your King, your Saviour, your great atonement. Why will ye so wilfully continue to be blind. God's Holy Scriptures are read by you, and were also read by your forefathers; but their false traditions misled them, and you continue to follow in their erring footsteps. Your false traditions have made you very unwise, oh ye children of Israel. Be wise now, and search diligently the Scriptures. Ye come of a wise stock, the wisest and best of all mankind of old, and ye will quickly understand that the same Messiah yourselves and your fathers long expected, was really crucified by your forefathers of old. God has abandoned you, refused to hear you, but for a time; the time now at hand, when, rousing yourselves, throwing aside your unwise stubbornness, you thoughtfully compare all prophecies concerning the Messiah that are in Holy Scripture, and so letting spiritual light into your minds, you find revealed that Jesus Christ was really the Messiah, and was really crucified by the children of Israel unwittingly through their false traditions. Yes, God will then hear your repentant wail, your despairing cry, that cry for which He and the crucified One have so long been listening, that cry which to you will express so much grief, will give great joy in heaven, that the long lost and scattered sheep of Israel have at last been found, found repentant, supplicating for pardon, through the great atonement of the Messiah, the Lamb of God. Then will you all rise as one man, as men who have long been blind, and suddenly restored to strong spiritual sight, and each girding up his soul, will with great energy and zeal, be patterns to all your Christian brethren, and spread far and wide God's Holy Word, and compel the unconverted, by perseverance, to understand it, and become God's holy children. Then will you once more become a nation, and take quiet possession of the land of your ancient fathers.

CHAPTER III.

THE RE-ORGANIZATION OF THE ONE OLD CHURCH OF CHRIST.

THE true universal Church of Christ is the Church of the Holy Scriptures—the Holy Scriptures as accepted by the Trinitarian Church of England, ignoring the traditions of men; ignoring also the opinions of all mankind who have lived since the days of the last of the Apostles—accepting the Holy Scriptures as the only spiritual guide, accepting them in their natural sense, not straining any portion to uphold this doctrine or that doctrine. It is a church of spiritual truth, of mutual kindness, of strong zeal in the holy cause of Christ, and of unity of purpose.

The church is a society, composed of the true worshippers of God, relying wholly upon the great atonement of the Messiah as their atonement, and accepting the Holy Scriptures as the only spiritual guide in the salvation of their souls, banding themselves lovingly together in accordance with the precepts of the Holy Scriptures, that they may worship God with unanimity of purpose, as it were with one voice, their holy supplications and their holy hymns of praise and thanksgiving ascending up to heaven continually, now here, now there, all round the earth, the church somewhere communing with God continually.

It is a society which, not content with winning a home in heaven for themselves, ardently desire that those not of their society should become members, and win a home for themselves also; ardently desirous of convincing the thoughtless and the ignorant of their great crime against the Almighty God, their Creator, and against the whole of mankind, in giving loose to evil thoughts and evil passions; and ardently desirous of instilling into them a right knowledge of the Holy Scriptures.

The church is an army of resolute aggressors, seeking out evil, and dragging it into the light, there exhibiting its vileness, and restraining it with firmness of purpose, warring not against the bodies of mankind, but warring against their spiritual ignorance, their thoughtlessness, their follies, and all injustice, especially towards the powerless poor.

The mission of the true Church of Christ is to inculcate spiritual truth, and dispel spiritual falsehood; to instil spiritual knowledge, and expel spiritual ignorance; to instil belief in God and in the Holy Scriptures, and expel disbelief; to inculcate a love of what is good, and abhorrence of all that is evil. To be matter of fact, than to indulge in flighty thoughts of the imagination; to be of the true church, rather than of a spurious sect; to follow the spirit of the Holy Scriptures in spiritual doctrine, rather than the imaginative doctrines of erring men; to rest in hope of happiness in heaven, rather than engross one's thoughts wholly upon the things of the world; to rely upon the mediatory death of Christ, in our supplications to God for pardon, rather than upon ourselves; to instil into everyone the great love of God and of His glorious Son for us, and the fervent desire of God that He should be enabled by our uprightness to carry us into heaven; to inculcate that all our distresses ensue wholly through sometimes our individual follies, and sometimes through the wickedness of mankind generally; to instil into every one the great truth that when anyone does wrongfully against God or against anyone of mankind, the wrong is felt also far off, like as when a stone is cast into still water disturbance is produced around; to teach all to obey just laws, rulers as well as the ruled; to uphold spiritual common sense and expel spiritual nonsense; to worship God aright and strive that everyone of mankind shall attain everlasting life in heaven; to habituate mankind to be right-minded, to substitute order in the nations in the stead of disorder; to favour perfect liberty to the well disposed, but firmly to restrain the evil disposed; to eradicate fraud and uphold honesty; to teach all mankind to cease strife and love peace; to set aside unjust laws, and substitute just laws; to be tended-hearted one towards the other, and be of one mind in the main spiritual things; to be generous and not niggardly in assisting the distressed, especially the well disposed; to be zealous in the cause of God, and not lukewarm; to abhor idleness and luxury; to love industry and sobriety; to be kind to the lesser creatures of the earth, and to cease destroying them for sport. This is the glorious mission of the true Church of Christ.

The strength of this great spiritual army is in proportion to the strictness of its discipline—the discipline being neither too rigid as to be irksome, nor so lax as to be disorderly—but like as every member of the church, being a child of God, restrains himself from doing evil in the sight of God, so he restrains himself from being captious, discontented, or ambitious towards the church; trampling on his own evil thoughts instantly they enter his mind, not requiring others to restrain him as do the godless, but restraining himself that the many spiritual soldiers may be disciplined into one strong united army—the clergy being the officers, the lay members as the rank and file, Christ upon his throne in heaven being their King and great commander—they his aggressive, holy, united army, in the final war of good against evil. These are the missions of the true church; missions, glorious to God, glorious to His Son our

Saviour and King, and a glorious occupation for all the children of God.

The Relation of the Church towards the State.

The church shall make laws for the governance in spiritual things, of its own members; every member shall honourably obey those laws—those of the nation not members of the church, shall not be suffered to interfere with the church in spiritual things. In spiritual things the church shall not obey them. No man not of the church shall have any authority in spiritual things over the church, for how is it possible that an unspiritual man can rule wisely in spiritual things; the interference of unspiritual men breeds disorder wherever it is suffered. The church shall not receive endowment from the state, but the church shall govern and maintain itself.

The church of the nation shall conform to the temporal laws of the nation; should any law be unjust the church shall persevere and strive by argument to have it rectified. The church of a nation shall assist in upholding the good rulers of that nation, but shall keep apart from evil rulers. With calmness, wisdom, and firm resolution, they shall not suffer any evil influence to be forced upon them; neither shall they force any laws of the church upon anyone not of the church. Perfect kindliness of heart, with active zeal in disseminating goodness, shall guide the church in its relation towards all mankind.

If two or more members disagree they shall not resort to the judges of the nation in any one thing, unless one of the disputants be not a member, the church discipline having no binding effect upon that one, the dispute may then be carried before the judges in the nation; but if the disputants are members of the church, they shall carry the cause to one of the judges appointed by the church; and they shall themselves, and not through advocates, state their case truly, as the children of God, as in the hearing of God; and the judge shall lovingly advise and arbitrate equitably between them, and his award shall be final—burying the dispute.

Unity in the Church.

God has not caused the Holy Scriptures to be written plainly, neither did he prompt the prophets to prophecy plainly, their sayings and writings are full of truth, as it were veiled, that in trying to unravel them mankind might usefully spend their life, and ever find them fresh; a mine of inexhaustible wisdom thinly veiled. God foresaw that familiar things would be almost unheeded, but unfamiliar things excite curiosity; that mankind would bestow little thought concerning the vast burning sun, the moon, the stars, and the other wondrous works of His, spread plainly throughout the world; but that a travelling sun, a comet, an unfamiliar thing, would excite the attention of all, yet not more marvellous than they. Therefore God in his wisdom thinly veiled by parable all things relating to the past, the present, and the future of man in the Holy Scriptures In like manner as the treasures of the earth are hidden in the earth, found only by those who diligently seek them; so the more thoroughly the Holy Scriptures are searched, the greater is the treasure found, in each a mine inexhaustible, and thus the mind of man is kept from flagging. Had God caused the Holy Scriptures to be written plainly, as that all His truths might, like the stars, be apparent at a glance, men's knowledge of those truths would have palled their minds, and like the alphabet of their own language be rarely thought of. The veiled riches of the Holy Scriptures, like those in the earth, beckon as it were everyone to seek for treasure. At first he scratches only upon the surface, and finds but little, perhaps becomes disheartened that all the treasure has not thereby been found, and being idle seeks no more, ever after foolishly believing that the earth has no treasure hidden in it. Whereas the true believer being earnest not captious, digs deeper and deeper still, every day finding fresh treasure, finding more the more he digs. It is therefore not possible that believers differing so greatly in acuteness should think alike, yet God accepts their worship if they be not idolaters, for God intended that each should exercise his soul in trying to unravel the parables. He has provided for them this spiritual occupation; errors of thought are made, but they are forgiven. He has given them perfect liberty to contemplate Him, however differently they may think; their souls meditating upon goodness thereby become sanctified. It is forgetfulness of God which brings condemnation on the souls of men, and not their difference of thought.

Deceive not yourselves; God having given perfect freedom to the mind of man, it is not possible that the thoughts of men concerning anything can be alike—they are not alike, each thinks differently from his neighbour, even in the simplest matter. Nay, many shall see a certain occurrence, and yet each will of necessity differ in his account of that occurrence; for the ramifications of thought are thousands of times ten thousand in number, therefore it is folly to expect to bring into uniformity all the thoughts of men; the efforts of mankind have always been in vain, however cruel in their coercion.

The Holy Scriptures teach that mankind sway themselves by two moving principles, good and evil—the one ensuring everlasting life, the other everlasting oblivion in the sight of God. All the good-disposed may be taught a right comprehension of

God, and be of one mind upon the four great doctrines of—
1. Love for God,
2. Love for Christ,
3. Love for the Holy Scriptures,
4. Love for mankind,

And joyfully be baptized as members of the true Church of Christ. Difference in opinion concerning the lesser doctrines giving joyous occasion of speaking and thinking of God, and not of engendering division; for the good-disposed, being spiritually wise, can comprehend that unity is a necessity, but uniformity of thought upon the lesser doctrines is not a necessity; no, nor yet exact uniformity upon the greater doctrines. To overcome a strong army that is against us, it is necessary that we should be stronger still. The strength of the well-disposed Christian army in the world to overcome the very strong evil-disposed army of the world consists in unity; separately the well-disposed are powerless, but with unity of spirit the evil-disposed army will melt like snow before the summer's sun. Hitherto the many evil-disposed—evil-disposed through ignorance of God—have been paramount, because hate to the few well-disposed united them more strongly than love one for the other among professing Christians. Henceforth the many sects shall comprehend they are but sects at loggerheads one with the other, because they are not truly the children of God, and that not one of them is the true Church of Christ. The well-disposed will cast aside their foolish notions, and they will come out of their many spurious churches untrammelled by aught; enriching themselves with love for God—love for His glorious Son—love for the Holy Scriptures, and love for all mankind; entering into the one true Church of Christ with zeal.

God has given great variety throughout the world, no two

things are exactly alike; nevertheless there is unity of purpose and harmony throughout all God's works. God does not intend that His children should do things alike, speak alike, think alike in all things, or eat and drink alike; but God does require them to supplicate for forgiveness of sins through the mediatory death of His glorious Son; furthermore He does require them to take the Holy Scriptures as their guide, and He does require them to love and assist one another in the spiritual war against the wickedness of mankind. God is graciously satisfied with these four bonds of union, whereby mankind become His children. The children of God must also be satisfied with these bonds of unity.

The wickedness that reigns throughout the world is continued by division among the children of God, through hypocrites separating them as it were into distinct sects or families. One family requiring as it were, every one of its members to have pale flesh, or hair of a particular colour, or head of a particular shape, or legs, arms, or feet of a particular form, or teeth possessing certain peculiarities, each sect foolishly refusing to commune with others not possessing those peculiarities, refusing to own them as brethren, looking upon them almost as a different species of man.

To hold back, to be outside the pale of His true church, to refuse to hold holy communion with the children of God, is to sin greatly—is not to be provided with the wedding-garment of brotherly love. The Lord, in parable, feasted the maimed, the halt, and the blind, at one great supper, not separating them, for their defects were veiled through their acceptance of the Lord's invitation; but there was one who, like the hypocrites, preferred singularity; he also presented himself, and showed, by not having on a wedding-garment, that he did not own the Lord's guests, all of whom had on the wedding-garment of unity, to be his brethren, prefering to stand aloof from them, therefore he was driven out with contumely by command of the Lord himself.

Remember always that a few united men are almost powerless for good, but many, having unanimity of purpose, may remove the greatest of all the mountains. In like manner, a sect is almost powerless for good. Rival sects fritter away all their power, neutralizing the good intentions one of the other, but their union as one church will enable them to do mighty things for the general welfare. Strive therefore to the very utmost, quickly to break down division; let everyone be no longer dissevered one from the other, and powerless, but zealously assist each other with unanimity of purpose. Hitherto you, oh sects, have set stubbornly your backs towards a central purpose, marching from it; now wheel yourselves about, and advance with your faces towards the *one* Church of Christ your glorious King, let that be your centre of unity.

Say not among yourselves, what saith this preacher or that preacher; but rather say, " What saith the Scriptures ?" for let it be widely known among you all, that many having authority, and many teachers, will strive strenuously, even through falsely interpreting the Scriptures, to keep you dissevered. Satisfied with their position, they will strive to prevent any change in your minds. Be watchful, therefore, and turn your backs on them. Let this be your answer : " Look around upon your nation, and behold the misery, the viciousness, and the spiritual ignorance of the people through disunion among the worshippers of God. We are almost powerless, therefore evil in all its forms is rooted in the habits of the people; we will no longer be disunited, but with unanimity of purpose and kindness of heart will form one church, and root out those evil habits, and habituate them to that which is just, holy, and good."

In the name of the Almighty God, and of His glorious Son our great atonement, you are now bidden to commune and hold spiritual fellowship with all the children of God, the members of the One Universal Church of Christ; their wedding garment is their holy bond of love and unity of purpose. Let not the Almighty God and His glorious Son see you without this wedding garment; for the time has come when God will distinguish those who are His children from those who are not, and he will declare those who hold back to be warring against Him. God desires to behold an army of united holy children, and not its scattered fragments.

Behold the seed has now been sown in the richest soil the earth affords; nevertheless the soil is very, very poor, yet the seed will sprout into a plant, and it will flourish, and man will not have the power to stop its growth, and it will overspread the earth, so that all the nations will nestle happily under it.

Celibacy of the Clergy.

It is not possible for a church of married clergy to be the one universal church over the whole earth, nor even over the whole of the nation. Of necessity it must be a lukewarm church, for married clergy are a perpetual weakness to a church, they are clerics who strive to unite God with the world, a thing impossible. Ofttimes they give themselves strongly to God, and almost ignore the world; at other times, being sorely tempted by family associations and cares, they give themselves strongly to the world, and almost ignore God. Their family cares and temptations are like weeds, choking more or less a promising plant; the plant would be a more goodly one were the weeds not there. Married clergy are as millstones to a zealous church; they are a great source of lukewarmness, discontent, and discord in a nation, for they are very burdensome to the weaklings of the people. The weaklings among the people are unwilling to bear the heavy yoke of the families of married clergy, in addition to the maintenance of all the schools and all the sanctuaries, so that the schools become insufficient, and the sanctuaries also; many of the people become neglected, and live without comprehending God, as do the heathen; the weaklings of the church become discontented and captious, seeing the lukewarmness of the married clergy, and the shameful ignorance of the people, and many separate themselves from the church and become as enemies. It is better to use the dedicatory offerings in maintaining many spiritual teachers than in maintaining many wives and their numerous children; and it is better that a spiritual teacher should devote himself wholly to spiritual things, than that he should take to himself a wife and be harassed and become worldly-minded through family cares. A sensuous man is utterly unworthy to be a spiritual teacher in the Church of Christ. It is better that the lay members should be satisfied that their dedicatory offerings are wisely expended in extending a right knowledge of God, than that they should be wasted upon sensuous men. If a spiritual teacher desire matrimony, let that teacher give place to another more worthy to be a servant of our God, and of His glorious Son; therefore the clergy shall vow before a congregation, in the sight of God, to live a life of strict celibacy while they continue spiritual teachers of the people, and they shall cease to be spiritual teachers should they fail to continue celibate. This shall be a perpetual decree of the One Church of Christ; it shall not be lawful for mankind to annul or amend it.

No longer shall the females be subordinate to male teachers in spiritual things, for hitherto men have signally failed to convince either the males or the females, but the females of the Church of Christ shall be equal in spiritual things to the males, that the intelligent of the males may concentrate their zeal in opening the understanding of the males, and the intelligent of the females perform the same estimable office to their own sex; for females are more amenable to the spiritual teaching of their own sex, and males to that of their own sex. Each sex shall have its own sanctuaries, its own spiritual teachers, schools, and institutions, set apart wholly to itself. Only to certain high spiritual male governors in the church shall the female teachers be subordinate, in all else the females of the church shall be equal in the sight of the church to the males of the church.

The Creed.

I believe the holy writers of the Scriptures were prompted by God the Almighty Creator and Governor of all things, to write them, therefore, I believe the Holy Scriptures to be true. I also believe the angel Jesus Christ came down from heaven, became man, suffered death for us, arose again, and ascended into heaven, where he reigns over the pardoned souls of the obedient who have preceded us into heaven, and over us his followers. I believe it the holy duty of all his children to obey him, worship him, to love and assist one another to the uttermost, and also to strive to teach all mankind to love, obey, and worhip him. Amen.

The creed of the church shall be unchangeable, nothing shall be added thereto, nor anything be taken therefrom. It shall be for ever the one universal creed.

CHAPTER IV.

THE RE-COMMENCEMENT OF THE TRUE CHURCH.

THE true Church of Christ has been in abeyance from the days of the last of the apostles until now, through the great errors of the Christians who came after. The good seed of the Word has now again been sown, and plenteous fruit will hereafter be produced.

Upon the whole earth there is not found one priest worthy to ordain any of mankind into the ministry of the true church, for all the nations, with their priests, have gone astray. The long lines of successive priests, some well disposed, others very evil, have taught great error, therefore they were but long lines of successive evil.

In the stead of a priest, two or more right-minded laymen shall, for this special occasion only, nominate one man, and one woman, right-minded like themselves, to be the first spiritual teachers in the church. The two or more laymen shall make it widely known in the nation, during four successive weeks, that upon a certain day in the fifth week, they, as the mouth-pieces of certain right-minded of mankind, will elect one man and one woman, to be the first spiritual pastors of the re-organized church. The males shall nominate the male, and the females shall nominate the woman, and their selection God will deem good; He will accept them as the leaders of His people. They shall afterwards assemble together, males and females, in their first sanctuary. In the sanctuary they shall have an altar, not an altar for sacrifice, for that is not needed in the Church of Christ, but an altar for dedicatory offerings unto God. They shall in the sanctuary abjure aloud all connection with the many spurious sects existing in the world ; then they shall, through one male and one female spokesman, as mouth-pieces of the congregation, nominate the selected ones to be the first ministers of the true Church of Christ. Immediately thereafter the selected ones shall together ascend upon the altar, and before the congregation, sprinkle themselves and one another with water, then suppliantly dedicate themselves aloud as zealous servants of God, to God, and they shall be the first ordained vicars of the true reorganized Church of Christ. The male vicar as the spiritual pastor of the males, and the female vicar as the spiritual pastor of the females. The males of the congregation of the choristers, and of the other officials of the sanctuary, shall also ascend the altar, and be baptized into the church by the male priest, and he shall suppliantly beseech God to accept them as sincere followers of the Messiah Christ, and themselves shall join aloud in the supplication and dedicate themselves to God, as zealous followers of His dear Son. The offerings shall then and hereafter always be laid upon an altar and dedicated to God for the service of the church ; preparatory to their being used, and out of the dedicatory offerings, the cost of the sanctuary shall be defrayed to the sureties. In like manner shall the female vicar afterwards baptize into the church, in the first female sanctuary, the females of her congregation, and dedicate themselves upon the altar to God, and the cost of their sanctuary be defrayed out of their dedicatory offerings.

The two vicars, and the baptized of those two first congregations, shall be accounted as very honourable afterwards in the church. The two vicars shall have authority, by reason of their office, to ordain others solemnly into the ministry ; none but those ordained by the constituted authorities in the church shall be empowered to appoint spiritual teachers or officials in the church, or be acknowledged by the church; for, like as men discipline their armies so shall the church be disciplined, that order and authority may reign throughout.

When twenty sanctuaries have been consecrated by the male vicar, each sanctuary having one rector and one curate, he shall appoint the most efficient of the rectors to be vicar over ten of the sanctuaries; and thereafter, until they have a bishop, for every ten sanctuaries there shall be appointed by the whole of the vicars an additional vicar. As it is with the males, so shall it be with the females.

When there are ten male vicars, they shall appoint, for this occasion only, one of their number to be their bishop, and he shall appoint and ordain, out of the rectors, one to fill the vacant vicarage. When there are ten more male vicars, the bishop shall appoint one out of the vicars to be a bishop, and the two bishops shall appoint one out of the rectors to the vacant vicarage. Then they shall separate the nation into two dioceses; one shall be bishop over one diocese, and the other the bishop over the other diocese. From time to time, as the church increases in growth, so they shall adjust the extent of the vicarage districts, both male and female, and for every additional ten male vicars the bishop shall appoint, as before, a vicar to be a bishop, and a rector to be vicar in his stead, the bishops separating the nation into dioceses, and adjusting the vicarages as they may deem necessary.

When there are ten bishops they shall appoint, for this occasion only, one of their number to be their archbishop, and the bishops shall nominate one of the vicars to fill the vacant bishopric. When there are twenty bishops, then the archbishop shall appoint out of the bishops another archbishop; and for every additional ten bishops the archbishops shall appoint, out of the bishops, an additional archbishop. From time to time, as the church increases, so shall the archbishops adjust their arch-dioceses. Every bishop in the sight of God is equal one to the other, and every archbishop is equal in the sight of God one to the other.

In changing a cleric from one office to another, the most zealous and fittest shall be selected; the welfare of the church shall be strictly kept in view, no undue favoritism shall be shown. The high officials of the church shall set a good example to the nation in this matter, and the whole church shall dutifully acquiesce, without any demur, in those acts of discipline.

The curates and school teachers of a sanctuary shall be appointed by the rector of that sanctuary; the rector of a sanctuary by the vicar of the district wherein that sanctuary is located—to vicarages vacant through death or other causes, by the bishop of that diocese, out of the rectors; to bishoprics vacant through death or other causes in an arch-diocese, by the archbishop of that diocese.

All the bishops and archbishops shall be males; the female spiritual teachers shall be subordinate to the bishops, but not to the lesser male priests.

From time to time the bishops and archbishops shall hold convocations to adjust the several districts necessitated by the growth of the church, and to adjust whatever else they may deem necessary; but they shall not effect any change unless it be very necessary, and their councils shall be brief and to the point. Their decision, and not their arguments, shall be published. They shall exhibit to the nation the great strength of their unity of purpose, and shall in that thing set a bright example to the nation.

Call not your sanctuaries by the name of church, for the true Church of Christ is not a sanctuary, but all the true followers of Christ; all his true followers throughout the whole world constitute his one church, Christ being the root and stem, the several national churches as the branches, like as the root, the stem, and the branches of a tree are one tree. Neither call yourselves the church of this nation or of that nation, but the Church of Christ in your nation, for the Church of Christ will cover the whole world, and not your nation only.

Disciplinary Rules of the Church.

The rector of a sanctuary shall control all the clerics attached to his sanctuary, the male rectors over the sanctuaries for males, and the female rectors over the sanctuaries for females. The minister of every sanctuary shall control and appoint all the school-teachers belonging to the schools of his sanctuary. So that all school-teachers and the curate shall be responsible to the rector, the males to the male rector, and the females to the female rector; all the rectors of a vicarage to the vicar, all the vicars of a diocese to their bishop, and all the bishops of an archdiocese to their archbishops; and the archbishops responsible to the whole church in the nation, to God, and to His beloved Son in heaven.

Every school-teacher and curate shall be thoroughly obedient to their rector, he to his vicar, the vicar to his bishop, the bishop to his archbishop, and he to the plain teachings of the Holy Scriptures, and to the rules of the church.

The rectors shall be called the convincers of the people, they shall be selected for their great ability in preaching to the people, convincing them of the truth of the Holy Scriptures; they shall be selected not merely for their oratory, but for their ability to convince. They shall not preach oftener than once in their own sanctuary every ten sabbaths, that the rectors and the congregations may alike be freshened. On the other nine sabbaths they shall preach in nine other sanctuaries appointed by their vicar; preaching the same words, or in modified words, for that which is strong in convincing one congregation is strong also in convincing others—their great aim shall be to teach plainly, briefly, and convincingly.

It is necessary that every cleric should read the Scriptures and the services, where read, thoroughly well and impressively, with a clear, strong voice, that every word may be caught by the whole congregation; and the bishops are enjoined not to ordain anyone deficient in these important requisites, and to displace for a time, or permanently, any clerics from ministering in the sanctuaries who may become inefficient, for the souls of the congregation must not be jeopardised through the ineffectiveness of any cleric. It is indispensable that the discipline of the church should not be in feeble hands; therefore let every archbishop, bishop, vicar, rector, curate, and school-teacher, resign the solemn trust his fellow-men have committed to his-care when sickness has incapacitated him from ministering to the people thoroughly well, and when he has attained the age of sixty years. Failing to resign, he shall be displaced. Let them be superannuated, receiving their yearly stipend in full until death.

The duty of the clergy is to officiate in the sanctuaries, in the ordinances of the church, and to take charge of the spiritual education of the members of the church; to minister to the sick, to counsel the distressed in mind, and to relieve the necessities of the true children of God. The church shall not suffer any worthy member to want food, shelter, or raiment; with special kindliness of heart shall their necessities be supplied. The rite of marriage, and the rite of infant baptism, shall be administered by the male clerics, and not by the female; but all female children above the age of one year shall be baptized by the female clerics.

The ambitious, the unscrupulous, and the promoter of discord among the clerics shall be at once deprived of his office for ever, as unworthy to be a spiritual teacher of the people. Neither the church, nor any part thereof, shall chronicle either his sayings or his doings, for he shall be accounted unworthy. Those who creep stealthily with a mask into the ministry shall be resolutely displaced by the bishop of their diocese instantly the mask is detected. The peace of the church shall be maintained. Through strict discipline of the clerics it shall be preserved.

P

Each one of the clergy shall be actively zealous, irreproachable, governing kindly but firmly; not permitting rebellion of subordinate clerics, neither permitting any other than their fellow-clerics to exercise authority in clerical matters, nor permitting clerics to interfere with the temporal government of the nation; working with the laity in a very kindly spirit where their active co-operation can be made available, and it can be very extensively—remembering that clerics and laymen, if children of God, are equal in His sight, their different positions being simply a mutual arrangement between man and man; the one undertaking zealously to devote himself to religiously instructing and guiding his fellows in the right way, and to lead them in the religious services; the laymen undertaking to provide the clerics with food, and the other necessaries that they may do so. Remembering that the clerical office must not be suffered to dwindle into an office of idleness and ease, as in the spurious churches, but be always full of active zeal in the mighty war of the true church against the many evils in the world.

God does not appoint the clerics, but He accepts their ministerings as leaders of the true church.

Numerous of the clergy, both male and female, shall be devoted wholly to missionary looking up of children for the schools, and for ministering spiritually to the sick in their own homes—for the conversion of all under error, and for spiritual advice to the godless, the careless, and the reckless—the male missionaries having the charge of all males, and the female missionaries of all females, who are not yet of the church, or who, through sickness, cannot attend the sanctuaries. Every sanctuary shall have missionaries labouring in the district of that sanctuary. They shall wear a distinctive costume; a plain dark blue outer robe, having embroidered thereon the ensign of the church, a plain black cross surmounted with the crown of glory in white; their headdress shall be black in colour. Let others of the clergy be teachers in the schools, and those educated for the ministry, but unordained, be their assistants.

The church shall establish schools to the very uttermost, for children will be the future perpetuators of the church; without them the church is weak, but with them in great numbers the church will become very strong.

The ministers shall baptize all who may sincerely desire to be baptized into the church, having the requisite knowledge, and being worthy—themselves and their children.

There shall be three orders in the church, separating the church into three divisions.

1. Those worthy ones who have been, and those who are sincere zealous workers of the church, these, both cleric and lay, are the saints of the true church; its very salt, the most highly esteemed by God of all His children—these only hold holy communion at the greater feast of unity.
2. Those between the ages of sixteen and twenty-one years, who being too young to assist at the greater feast of unity, are deemed worthy to hold holy communion at the lesser feast of unity.

3. Those who are below the age of sixteen years, also those not having a right knowledge, the lukewarm, the careless, the idle, and the unworthy.

It shall not be lawful for males, other than bishops and archbishops, to enter the sanctuaries for females during religious service, nor be present at the Lord's table with them; nor lawful for females to enter the sanctuaries for males during religious service, other than at the rite of marriage, and at the rite of infant baptism, nor be present at the Lord's table with them; the female spiritual teachers shall thickly veil the face when among men—only in the presence of bishops or archbishops shall they unveil.

The ordained clerics, male and female, when not officiating in the sanctuaries, shall wear comfortable habits, distinguishing them from the laity, of a fashion suited to the climate, from which they shall not deviate; from the highest to the lowest the fashion and the colour shall be alike; the colour shall be like to the blue of the sky, that of the unordained clerics dark blue, plain, and all of one colour, girt about the loins. The covering for the head shall be deep blue. They shall not wear rings upon their fingers, nor ornament of any kind, nor suffer any emblem or symbol upon their persons or their sanctuaries, excepting only the ensign of the church, a plain black cross surmounted with a crown of glory embroidered in white. This ensign shall be embroidered six inches in length, from the bottom of the cross to the top of the crown of glory, upon each breast of the habit; it shall not be of greater size upon any of the habits at any time.

The ministering habits of the archbishops shall be white, embroidered with gold-colour thread, not profusely, but sufficient to distinguish their office from that of the bishops, whose ministering habits shall also be white, slightly embroidered with gold-colour thread. The ministering habits of the lesser clergy shall be plain white; and the habits of the choristers shall also be plain white; upon each breast shall be the ensign of the church, a plain black cross surmounted with the crown of glory in gold-colour thread.

All the ordained and unordained clerics of a sanctuary shall take their plain, satisfying meals, and live in one house together, the males and females in separate houses; each shall be provided with two rooms, plainly but comfortably furnished, that comfortably and socially they may reside together, and yet be not over-burdensome to their people; male servitors shall serve the males, and female servitors the females.

A separate house shall be provided for every vicar, every bishop, and archbishop. The vicar shall not have more than two servitors, a bishop not more than three, an archbishop not more than four.

The archbishop shall be esteemed, in the sight of the church, supreme over the chiefs of the nation in spiritual things, and their equal in temporal things.

Every cleric ministering in a sanctuary, and the superannuated below the office of a bishop, shall have the word "Reverend" prefixed to the name, and every bishop and archbishop shall have the words "Very Reverend" prefixed to his titular appellation. When a bishop or archbishop is addressed, he shall be addressed like as a rector is addressed, with great respect, but without servility. Christ only is Lord of His Church, and there are no lesser lords.

Every vicar shall be an honorary judge, advising and arbitrating upon all matters in dispute between lay members in his vicarage, or between the clerics and lay members; to the advice or award of the vicar they shall defer. If one of the disputants should reside in one vicarage, and another of the disputants in another, then the two vicars shall unitedly consider and arrange the matter. The male vicars shall adjudicate when the disputants are males, and the female vicars when they are females. When disputes arise between male and female lay members, the male vicars shall be arbitrators; and where disputes arise between male and female clerics, then the bishops of their respective dioceses shall be the arbitrators. It shall be considered dishonourable to prefer the judgment of a judge who is not a member of the church. A vicar, being also an arbitrator in things temporal, shall have a rector to assist him in his spiritual duties.

Should either of the disputants be dissatisfied with the award of the vicar, then the dispute shall be carried before the bishop of the diocese; but it shall not be accounted honourable to the dissentient thus to trouble the peace of the church; the children of God should strive to ensure peace, and not cause trouble.

The church shall not suffer any member to be oppressed or injured wilfully by those not of the church; his fellow members near by shall resolutely succour him to their very utmost; the just cause of that one shall be the cause of the whole church of the nation; resolutely oppression shall be resisted; the voice of the whole church shall be centred in the rulers of the church, they shall be the mouthpieces of the church, and all the members shall uphold them. The members shall not take upon themselves one to consider himself to be at liberty to do this thing, another to do that thing, but, like the soldiers of a well disciplined army, the voice of the rulers shall be to them as words of command to be obeyed, and not criticised, that their words may have great weight in the nation.

Every bishop shall appoint in his diocese a lay member of the church, learned in the laws of the nation, who shall carry before the judges of the nation every act of wrong, of oppression, and of wilful injury to any member in the diocese, committed by those not of the church. The act shall not be exaggerated, but plainly and with strict truth it shall be brought before the judge. It shall be accounted very dishonourable to exaggerate or lie in the matter; the children of God shall not in that thing imitate the godless advocates.

Should any member of the church be unruly, and persist in setting at naught the admonitions of the rulers of the church, they shall cause his name to be expunged from the rolls of the church, and it shall be deemed dishonourable in the sight of God for members thereafter to hold social fellowship with him; they shall abhor him, like as they shall abhor the liar and the fraudulent. If he repent, and the rulers of the church be satisfied with the sincerity of his repentance, he may again be restored into the church.

The Ensign of the Church.

This shall be an Ensign unto you, that ye may distinguish your brethren, the children of Christ, from those who are not his children. Upon your sanctuaries, upon the habits of your spiritual teachers, and upon the dress of all the workers of the church, and upon the dress of all those in the seminaries and institutions of the church, and upon the dress of all who congregate at the Lord's Feast of Unity, and at the love feasts; upon all the hymnals, psalters, devotional books, the Holy Scriptures, and upon all printed announcements of the officials of the Church of Christ, there shall be a Cross surmounted

by a Crown of Glory; the former commemorating the sufferings of Christ for us, the other commemorating his present glory. The one shall not be used without the other. No other ensign shall you have upon your sanctuaries, upon your houses, upon the habits of your teachers, or upon aught else. That ensign of our Lord, the King Christ, shall be to you a visible rallying point, a bond of union; you shall not at any time disgrace it in the eyes of anyone, but they shall deem it honourable through the uprightness and kindness of heart yourselves the bearers thereof entertain towards mankind, especially towards those who are brethren in Christ; but in no part of the interior of the sanctuary, nor in the school-house, nor in any house, shall the ensign be fixed. What the crescent is to the Mahometan so this ensign shall be to you, a visible rallying point.

Seminaries.

The children of the church, from six to fourteen years of age, shall be educated in seminaries set aside by the church; they shall all be taught alike. The foundation of their knowledge shall be the Holy Scriptures. They shall be habituated to uprightness of conduct, they shall not be debarred from recreation, for innocent recreation is very good in all of mankind, it is only that which is not innocent that is to be shunned. The best behaved, that are learned in the Scriptures and good readers, shall be further educated in other seminaries, that they may become spiritual teachers of the people; there shall be no undue favour shown, but the best behaved good readers, that are learned in the Scriptures, shall alone be selected, whether their parents are rich or poor; the church shall educate and provide for them in this thing, the church shall do its duty continually. They shall be considered the flower of the youth of the nation.

Children under fourteen years of age shall not be robbed of their birthright to be educated, they shall not be neglected nor set to work for their livelihood; they shall not be forced into ignorance, through being forced into servile work.

From among the best conducted of the male and female poor of the schools, not set apart for the ministry, shall, at the age of fourteen years, be selected those who desire to be servitors; they shall be taught the necessary duties of servitors, or of some handicraft, until the age of sixteen years, when the office of servitor or of the handicraft shall be provided for them.

The selected youth of both sexes intended for the ministry, shall be educated until the ages of twenty-one years, in all manner of useful knowledge, in the sciences, the principles of law and equity, the art of oratory, the art of singing in unison, and the simple remedies of the physician and surgeon. Those selected for foreign missions shall also be taught the language of the country for which they are destined. At the age of twenty-one years they shall be appointed teachers in the home schools, and as vancancies occur, from those intended for the home ministry shall be selected the most fluent of speech, the best readers, those strong in health, and the best conducted, to be curates; and from the residue shall be selected those whose office shall be to read out of the Holy Scriptures, and explaining them to the sick of the people; and from the residue some shall be fully taught the art of the physician and the surgeon; and some shall be teachers in the schools; they shall all be accounted clerics, and wear the blue honourable habits of clerics, and each shall have embroidered on the breast of the habit the ensign of the church.

The church in every nation shall strive to the uttermost to carry to nations, having a less knowledge of God, a right comprehension of Him; therefore, for every ten sanctuaries, the church shall educate and maintain, until the age of twenty-one years, one well disposed intelligent male, and one intelligent female of a foreign nation; they shall be considered like to your own people, and at the age of twenty-one years they shall be appointed assistants to the missionaries of their own people; they shall be accounted clerics of the church, and wear the blue habits of clerics, and have embroidered on the breast of the habits the ensign of the church. Until the several nations are well grounded in a right knowledge of God and in general education, shall the church, in an intelligent nation, maintain and educate those intended as missionaries.

Self supporting schools and colleges shall also be established away from towns, distributed throughout the nation, in connection with the church, which shall be under the supervision of the vicar in whose district they may be located.

Missions.

Christ died not for a few but for all who call upon his name, worshipping his Father, the God and Creator of all things. The Messiah has commanded his followers, the church, to be very zealous, and to spread the good tidings of the Gospel in every nation, convincing them of its truth, that all mankind may become his followers, and enter heaven, where he is. A lukewarm church, in the sight of God, is a failure in that it fails to bring the nations to the feet of Jesus; it fails to convince the nations of the truth of the good tidings of the Messiah; she idly locks the treasure within her bosom, from sheer want of love towards Christ and towards mankind—the good tidings she only weakly believes, and therefore she only weakly acts; she is only lightly prized in heaven, for she lacks the one thing needful, zealous faith. Be ye not thus unworthy, but throw all the united strength of your strong zeal first upon the people of your own nation, strive your uttermost to make plain to them the mighty plan of God ; let that plan be to you as an alphabet, the groundwork of all spiritual knowledge, then they will clearly understand the mission of Christ from heaven to earth, and being convinced they will become an upright people ; then will their uprightness be as a shining light before your missionaries abroad, and great will be their success among the nations—take special heed and be not like those bewilderers—the spurious clerics who preach bewildering nonsense to their flocks, year after year, teaching them nothing ; but teach frequently the mighty plan of God, until like their own alphabet they have thoroughly mastered it, then will the Holy Scriptures be ever afterwards to them a mine of great spiritual wealth and a great comfort.

The archbishops shall lay aside a portion of the church funds for foreign missionary purposes ; they shall appoint the missionaries, and uphold effectively at home a foreign missionary institution, that foreign missionary efforts may be thoroughly assisted.

Ye shall not call yourselves Protestants, but Christians, for your priesthood comes not out of the Papacy, nor do you protest against the Papacy, for she is not a Christian church but a spurious church, being only part Christian, a greater part idolatrous, and a greater part still unscriptural ; therefore the true church does not protest against her, nor against the church of Mahomet, but ignores the Papacy altogether as a Christian church ; ignoring also the other spurious churches, by whatever name they are called.

It shall be the great aim of the church in every nation to habituate every one of her members to perfect uprightness, in the sight of God and in the sight of man, causing them always to cherish in their minds that each is a member of the whole holy family of God upon earth—each assisting the other in all good things to the uttermost.

Behold, ye women, faithful followers of the Lord Christ, into thy hands God gives thy sex, to teach them His Word, and to teach and love them as thy sisters, and to teach them to love and cherish each other as children of the most High God. The Messiah, thy King, desires that thou shouldest win all thy sex to God, for behold the time has now come when throughout the world female man shall no longer be oppressed. Thy gentleness employ usefully and largely, for behold thy sex also have become spiritual soldiers of the King Christ, and do thou thy part well and perseveringly.

The spiritual teachers, male and female, shall not be ignorant of the art of the physician, and certain women shall be instructed in midwifery, that they may minister to the simple bodily ailments of the people; the males ministering to the males, the women to those of their own sex. Neither shall they be ignorant of the just law of equity, that they may rightly arbitrate in the disputes of their people. Neither the spiritual teachers, nor the sisterhoods, shall take any reward from mankind; but for love towards God and towards mankind, they shall do their uttermost. And some shall not be ignorant of the musician's art, that, upon an instrument of music, the most skilful may fitly lead the congregation.

The active women of the church shall also occupy themselves in educating the young females of the nation, in tending the sick, reading to the sick and aged, looking after the welfare of their sex, and in worshipping God and His glorious Son. It shall be accounted very dishonourable for any female of the church to be idle when in sound health, or to do aught that is dishonourable to her sex. The married shall tend their little ones thoroughly, but their little ones shall not engross all their thoughts, to the exclusion of God. They shall teach their little ones how to pray, and the unmarried shall assist mothers in their duties, that the mothers may not be as slaves, for it is honourable for the laity both to be married and to be chaste. It is dishonourable in the sight of God for a member of the true church to marry one who is not a member, for it shows a backward step.

Let there be temporary retreats for the distressed in mind, for widows, and for the aged, that their thoughts may be spiritually homeward, loving and honouring them as members of the family of God. But the young and the strong must be active and zealous soldiers of their King, the Lord Christ; battling resolutely against wickedness in every form; battling against their own individual temptations, and the evil ways of the evil-disposed; convincing them by precept and by example to do good and to abhor all that is evil. For idleness, when there is so much spiritual work ready to their hand, is a great crime in the sight of God. Their active service is honourable, but idleness is dishonourable.

There shall be established hospitals and dispensaries in common for the members of the church and for those not of the church.

From among the widows in the church there shall be selected holy, capable women, by the oldest female rector in every vicarage, to act as midwives to the people, whether of the church or not of the church; they shall be taught thoroughly their art, and they shall have the assistance, when necessary, of a female medical practitioner. Houses wherein they shall be lodged and maintained shall be provided for them, and for each there shall be appointed two rooms, plainly and comfortably furnished, and a skilful female medical practitioner of mature age shall be over each house, in unison with a female cleric. The sisterhood of midwives shall be habited in dark brown robes, with the ensign of the church embroidered on the breast.

Let there be also a house in every vicarage, for the residence together, in bonds of holy love, of a limited number of unmarried and widowed holy women, to be employed, some in tending as nurses the sick in the vicarage district, both male and female, who are dangerously ill, and as Scripture readers to the sick. This sisterhood of holy nurses shall be habited in robes of a light brown colour, having embroidered on the breast thereof the ensign of the church. A cleric of mature age shall be over each house.

The lay members of the church shall strictly subject themselves to the rules of the church; they shall consider it dishonourable in the sight of men and of heaven wilfully to disobey them. They are as the rank and file of a well-disciplined army, each an unit in a glorious family, each adding honour and glory when right-minded, but dishonour and shame if evil-minded. Let no man feel aggrieved without good cause, let him not disturb the peace and harmony of the church, for if truly children of God they will be loving and forbearing, and strive to restrain their own weaknesses, and overlook the slight weaknesses of others. If they strive not, then they are not really children of God, but children of the world; bearing always in mind, that the children of God cannot do without producing much evil what is not noticed in the wicked, for the wicked are expected to do and talk wickedly; but upon the members of the Church of Christ the eyes of the wicked, the wavering, and the weak in faith are fixed, influencing them sooner or later greatly. The members shall be honest, straightforward, truth-tellers, not tale-bearers, chaste, sober, righteous, slow to anger, forgiving, in all their dealings giving the preference to those like-minded as themselves, that mutually they may assist each other.

Innocent amusements shall not be debarred, but they shall not engross too much of their thoughts, lest they be led to forget God; but in moderation they are good, in that they satisfy the innocent longings of the body.

The rules of the church shall not be binding for more than one generation of thirty years, for it shall be deemed incapable that one generation shall bind another in anything. It is the birthright of every generation of thirty years to ratify, revoke, or amend, through their representatives in solemn convocation, the rules of the previous generation of thirty years. Therefore, every thirty years there shall be a holy convocation of the church. Seven of the representatives shall be elected by the lay communicants, five by the several orders of the clergy, and one shall be elected by the archbishops out of the archbishops, and he shall preside at the convocation, which shall be dissolved within one month after its assemblage, otherwise it shall not have the power to confirm, add to, or revoke, but the rules of the previous era of thirty years shall be considered as confirmed. A spirit of mutual love, kindliness of heart, and unpresumption, with an entire absence of party spirit, shall govern their hearts; and their deliberations shall not be made known, nor be written down; their decisions only shall be made known to the church, which shall accept their award as final. for the ensuing term of thirty years, without recrimination or criticism. The rules of one age shall not be altered unless they be absolutely necessary, for frequent alterations are frequent evils.

The first year of every century shall be a year of jubilee to the whole church throughout the world; it shall be a year of unity among the followers of Christ throughout the world; there shall be an interchange of courtesy, of holy communion and fellowship among the nations. And there shall be a holy assembly, during three months, of archbishops from every nation, in the chief city of that nation—in the spring time of that nation—which numbers the greatest number of the children of Christ. And the children of Christ in that nation shall with open hearts and great love entertain and lodge them, and claim them as fellow-heirs of Christ; and when they depart, it shall be with great honour, and with the solemn blessing of the archbishops of the honoured nation. And at the convocation the archbishops shall commune together, and confer together concerning their respective rules, that each may learn from the other the right governance of the church.

All the sanctuaries, buildings, moneys, goods, and chattels vested or bought for the use or with the moneys of the church shall be considered vested in the archbishops of their nation, in behalf of the true church in that nation. They shall be the chief judges in all things appertaining to the governance of the church, from whose judgment there shall be no earthly appeal. They shall have the fullest power to bind and loose all things relating to church governance; to them the children of God shall defer, both clerical and lay, as being for the eternal benefit of all the church.

CHAPTER V.

THE FEAST OF UNITY.

LIKE as spurious clerics have bewildered themselves with the lying doctrine of the Trinity, even adopting the foolish Athanasian creed as their creed, so have they bewildered themselves concerning the Last Supper of the Messiah; they have become bewilderers of the people rather than teachers.

The Feast of Unity is a feast observed only by the zealous followers of Christ, instituted by our Lord as their bond of union, common to all who believe his great atonement to be their atonement before God, his God and our God. The feast is a gathering together of the zealous workers of the Great King, whereat they eat and drink together in commemoration of his last supper, strengthening each other in mutual love and social fellowship, because of their unity of spirit in looking forward to their final redemption through the mediatory death of their Great Atonement. It is a feast whereat it is lawful only for the zealous workers, cleric and lay, and for the aged and infirm who have been zealous workers, to sit together, for they only are the saints of the church, the most worthy ones of the earth; the lukewarm and the unbeliever are not worthy, nor the disorderly. Therefore the saints of the church are not merely believers and worshippers, but zealous workers also; in the sight of God they are esteemed greatly, for they are truly His working children, the winners of souls, and the children of the Lord Christ their King, and the true friends of all mankind.

The twelve apostles of the Messiah were the first saints of the true church; with them Christ held holy communion, and they with Christ, friends one of the other, united strongly together through their love of God, he their teacher, they his pupils. Knowing that his mediatory death would take place on the morrow, the Messiah urged them occasionally to meet together, and continue in the same unity of spirit after his death, ordaining that all his followers should meet and partake of food together in holy bonds of unity of purpose and mutual love, thereby commemorating his mediatory death and strong desire for their unity, that they might be strong in the warfare waged by his church against the wickedness of evil men. Therefore, twelve times during each year the Feast of Unity shall be held in every sanctuary. There shall first be held a service of one hour; then all the saints shall partake of food, many taking out of one platter and many out of one cup, as a token of unity of spirit. This they shall do in commemoration of the unity of spirit that swayed the right-minded at the table of our Lord and King the Messiah, and also in commemoration of his great love for mankind in pouring out his blood and giving up his body to be broken for us; that through his mediatory death our souls might be pardoned, and enter heaven. Then shall the minister give to the congregation an account of his own labour, and of the zealous workers of the church of his district in extending and strengthening the kingdom of their Lord since their previous assemblage; and, with praise and thanksgiving to their God and to His glorious Son their King, end each feast.

A lay saint shall be admitted to Holy Communion only at the sanctuary where he habitually worships. If he does aught that is dishonourable, the minister of his sanctuary, when the same is made known to him, shall admonish him If he again transgress, he shall be suspended from holding Holy Communion, nor shall he again be deemed a saint until he thoroughly repents. When a member becomes a saint by admittance to Holy Communion with saints, and afterwards habitually worships elsewhere, the minister of his former sanctuary shall give him a certificate of his saintship; it shall be to him a sign of his honourable conduct, and to the minister of his present sanctuary, to whom it shall be permanently given.

By saints alone shall the several offices of the church be filled, from the humblest to the most exalted, and they shall be held in mutual honour, for there are none so honourable among the rest of mankind.

Like as the ordinance of baptism separates those who are members of the church from those who are not members, so in like manner the ordinance of the Lord's Supper distinguishes the true servants of God and of His Messiah from those whose love for God is not very strong—not so strong as to work for Him. All are servants who unitedly work to extend the kingdom of Christ upon earth, whether as ministers, as teachers in the schools, or in ministering to the necessitous both of body and soul, or in striving to spread around a right comprehension of God. These are the servants of God and of His Messiah; these are the saints, the active workers of the one Church of Christ.

CHAPTER VI.

THE SANCTUARY.

LET there be in every sanctuary seats free to all. Let no seats be enclosed, for the Church of Christ is the church of all, equally for the poor as well as for the rich. God looks only for the worship of the contrite in heart.

Be very zealous until there be in every diocese throughout your nation one sanctuary for every one thousand souls of the population, and take especial heed and imitate not the foolish and idolatrous sects, who build a few sanctuaries for the glorification of man, but foolishly pretend them to be for the glorification of God. Lavish not your means upon ornamented bricks and stone, for God, the creator of the starry skies, values not those things, but provide sanctuaries sufficient in number.

The sanctuaries shall be plain, neat, and cheery within, and neat on the outside, without meanness, and without ostentation, and shall be maintained very clean and suitably. There shall be no symbols, for these are oft the stepping stones to folly; nor images, nor pictures, nor monuments, nor tablets for the glorification of man in your sanctuaries. Coloured glass may be used, but no symbol or representation thereon of any living or supposed living creature. A decorated sanctuary God does not deem dishonourable, but it is more honourable to provide sufficient sanctuaries and schools, and to administer to the wants of the necessitous of His children.

There shall be no sacrificial altar in the sanctuary. An

altar indeed is needed, but not for sacrifice, but to receive the thank and dedicatory offerings of the people to God. The altar shall have railings upon it on three sides. At baptism the little child shall be placed upon the altar, and dedicated by his guardians to God; and his guardians shall solemnly undertake, as far as in them lay, to cause him to live uprightly and honestly before God. And at the age of fifteen years, upon certain convenient days, the children shall, of their own free will, release their guardians, and upon the altar dedicate themselves aloud to God as followers of the Holy Christ their King. And upon the altar all converts shall likewise dedicate themselves to God ; and all who are appointed as teachers of the young and spiritual teachers of the people, at their ordination. Also when curates become rectors, when rectors become vicars, when vicars become bishops, and when bishops become archbishops, they shall renew the dedication of themselves to God, as followers of the Holy Christ. And upon the altars shall be placed all the gifts dedicated for the maintenance of the church in the nation, and of all things connected with the sanctuary; nothing shall be used of the gifts until they be solemnly placed upon an altar, and solemnly offered and dedicated to the service of God. It shall be unlawful for the clerics to use any gift until it be first solemnly placed upon an altar, and prayerfully offered to God and His glorious Son our King.

Dedicate your sanctuaries to God and His glorious Son; call them not after the name of any other living being. Distinguishing them one from the other after this manner :—

The Sanctuary of the Holy God—of the Messiah—of the Holy Ghost—of the One God—of the Almighty—of the Wondrous God—of Christ—of Jesus—of the Great Atonement—of the All-sufficient Atonement—of Our Kind Deliverer—of the Just One—of Good Things—of the All-seeing God—of

Pleasant Things—of Holiness—of Goodness—of God's Love—of Spiritual Love—of Redemption—of Sanctification—of Truth—of Wisdom—of Praise—of Thanksgiving—of Faith—of Prayer—of Good Will—of Newness of Life—of the Lord of Hosts—of the Creator—of Jehovah—of Emmanuel—of Salvation—of Holy Joy—of the Everlasting God—of the Word of God—of the Holy Scriptures—of the Voice of God—of the Spirit of Christ—of the Spirit of the Holy Scriptures—of the Mighty Councillor—of the Great High Priest—of the Children of God—of the Children of Christ—of Temperance—of the True of Heart—of Equity—of Justice—of Obedience to God—of Spiritual Light—of Spiritual Discipline—of Eternal Life—of Mercy—of Forgiveness—of Repentance—of Contrition—of the Strong in Faith—of the Blessed—of a Right Understanding—of a Right Knowledge—of the Commandments—of a Right Spirit—of the Humble—of the Meek—of the Saved—of Our Everlasting Home—of Benevolence—of Charity—of Mutual Love—of Spiritual Unity—of Mutual Help—of Patience—of the Contented—of the Zealous—of True Worshippers—of the Holy Father—of the Holy Son—of the Only Born Son of God—of the Corner Stone—of the Master—of the Son of David—of the Son of Man—of Unity of Faith—of Holy Brotherhood—of Fidelity—of the Great King.

Names given only to distinguish one sanctuary from another—names the one equal to the other—every sanctuary being dedicated to the One Holy God and His Holy Son, the Christ our King. Therefore is every sanctuary equal in the sight of God.

Call not your sanctuaries by the appellation of churches, but call them sanctuaries.

CHAPTER VII.

Religious Services.

THE services shall be as that in the Trinitarian Church of England. Those portions which are contradictory to the true Scripture doctrines shall be modified by the clergy according to their judgment. They shall read the services distinctly in their natural tone of voice, and the hymnal tunes shall be such as are easy for all the people, and the people shall be taught to sing in like manner as they are taught to read. Prayer, praise, and thanksgiving being sometimes addressed to God, and sometimes to His glorious Son. Beseeching the granting of every prayer wholly through the great atonement of Jesus Christ our Messiah, for without him there is no deliverance from condemnation, and like as God desires that we may love and obey Him, it is also good when we supplicate that not only ourselves, but all mankind also, may love and obey His holy commandments, and be protected from all things hurtful to both soul and body.

It is good to diversify the services with prayer, praise, and thanksgiving, the minister taking part, and the people responding with the natural voice, that the strong and weak of hearing may understand every word and unite in giving utterance, varying with hymns and psalms. With the reading of portions of Scripture by the minister, and with clear explanation and exhortations. But neither his explanations nor his exhortations shall be long, lest they be wearisome to the people and bewilder rather than teach.

It is good to have a choir to lead the people in their songs, and it is good to let them be simple and easy, that their thoughts may not dwell too much upon the tunes, lest their songs proceed not from the heart but only from the lips

Let certain of the choir sometimes take one part, and the residue of the choir and the congregation make responses, for it is very wise to stir the hearts of the worshippers, that their souls may pour forth utterances and be maintained full of wakefulness, for a monotonous service begets drowsiness in the lukewarm; these a diversified service stirs up, and quickens their understanding, and the services become to them a pleasure, and not a duty that is wearisome. But eschew the superstitious changing of dresses, theatrical genuflections, and swinging of censers, for these are folly and lead to greater follies. Remembering that a cleric is simply one of the congregation, neither more nor less; more highly esteemed in the sight of God only when he is more worthy than any there.

Every spiritual teacher shall read in his natural tone of voice, very clearly, and impressively. It is necessary that the services shall be so plain to the understanding as that children may be able to take part in all the responses, and in the singing of the hymns and psalms; and let the hymnals and psalters throughout the nation be alike, that a traveller may find himself at home in every sanctuary he enters.

Let music be used in the sanctuary, not merely to tickle the ear, or to gratify the vanity of any of the choir, or to exhibit the skill of the musician, but solely for the glorification of God and His dear Son; nevertheless, let not the music give forth uncertain sounds, but be thoroughly well played. It is the stirred souls of the worshippers, and not simply their melody, that is so estimable in the sight of God—the cry, the sobs of the penitent broken heart, is the music God loves most to hear.

Every Sabbath Day there shall be two services. The commemorative natal day of the Messiah, the commemorative day of his great atonement, and the commemorative day of his ascension shall be as the Sabbaths. On every other day there shall be at least one service.

There shall be an offertory after every service; the offerings of the females shall be devoted to the maintenance of their spiritual teachers, their schools, and sanctuaries; the offerings of the males shall in like manner be devoted to the maintenance of their teachers, their schools, and sanctuaries, and to the maintenance of the bishops, archbishops, and foreign missions.

Holy Days.

The natal day of the Holy Christ our King, shall be a day of great rejoicing, of praise, and thanksgiving in the sanctuaries, with joyful hymns. It shall be a day of holy rejoicing, and of holy communion.

The day of crucifixion, that sad day, shall be observed as a day of mourning and penitential prayer; mourning that the unholiness of Adam rendered necessary the mediatory death of the Messiah. The songs shall be mournful, the sanctuaries be draped with mourning cloths, as though his death were but yesterday. It shall be a day of mourning, a day of fasting, and holy communion.

The commemorative day of the ascension of our King shall be a day of holy rejoicing, with joyous songs of praise and thanksgiving, and there shall be holy communion on that day. It shall be a joyous day, commemorating the victory of our Deliverer, as it were yesterday, over the great temptations of the world, and therefore of our redemption through his great victory.

These days of commemoration shall be on week days, and not on the Sabbath. When they fall on the Sabbath Day, then shall they be commemorated on the day following. The church shall wholly abstain from servile work, themselves and their cattle, on those days.

The natal day of every child of God shall also be observed as a day of praise, and family thanksgiving privately, with joyful hymns, because of the heavenly inheritance.

There shall also be a day of harvest thanksgiving to God, for His continued providence in providing food and sustenance for all His creatures. It shall be a day of holy communion, and a day of rejoicing; it shall be a day of rest to the beasts of burden, and a double allowance shall be given them.

Festivals.

It is good that the children of God should not be as strangers one to the other; it is good that they should socially meet together and hold kindly fellowship one with the other; therefore, five times every year, for about one hour, the elders of a congregation; those above the age of twenty-one years, and the married, shall provide a simple repast in honor of their pastor, and of all the teachers in connection with the sanctuary. The feast shall be held in a school-room, and the pastor shall select some of the young and active to the honourable office of tending at the repast. And five times every year, for about one hour, the young of the congregation who have been confirmed, up to the age of twenty-one years, shall provide a simple repast in honour of their pastor, and of all the teachers in connection with their congregation. And twice every year, for about one hour, a simple repast shall be given to the children of the schools in connection with their sanctuary by the pastors and teachers in connection with their sanctuary—the males having their feasts by themselves, and the females by themselves. The rich shall not keep apart from the poor, but they shall commingle, and the teachers shall commingle with them; and the Holy Spirit of God will rest upon them, and kindliness of heart, and the Spirit of Christ shall be theirs. Every congregation shall have, in like manner, these feasts of mutual love, alternating with the holy feasts of unity; and the congregation shall purify their bodies, and habit themselves very cleanly, for at their feasts the Holy Spirit of God will love to be in their midst.

CHAPTER VIII.

The Voice of Warning.

THE church shall not suffer herself to relax in her vigilance. She shall not, at any time, suffer her ministers to become careless, or pretentious, or superstitious; nor suffer a married priest to continue in the ministry, nor a sensuous one; nor suffer any of her priests to encroach or be presumptuous, or to create division among the congregation placed in his charge; nor suffer the children to be defrauded of their right to be thoroughly well educated; nor suffer those not of the church to interfere with the discipline of the church. The church shall set always before her a high standard of excellence, and she shall not suffer it to be lowered, lest great sorrow, great dissension, and great misery fall upon the whole world; for, like as a strong army continues strong while subject to good discipline, so shall the church—it is not possible that lax discipline, and an efficient church can co-exist—good and evil will not pull together; therefore, with great kindness, great love, and great resolution of purpose, shall the church keep her heart. She shall grow in love, in holiness, in unity; peace and holy joy shall be hers; her people shall become glorious in the sight of our God and of Christ our glorious King, and restrain resolutely all tendency to do or think evil.

CHAPTER IX.

THE nations of the whole world are steeped in great anxiety, poverty, and spiritual ignorance, because they, like their predecessors, have not understood aright the spirit of the Holy Scriptures, else they would not have submitted themselves to spiritual nonsense, nor would they have conceived the injustice, oppression, violence, and evil which abound in every nation to be irremediable. The nations have swung themselves into a whirlpool of error through the disobedience of Adam, and afterwards through their own spiritual ignorance and brutishness. They must, through strong effort, swing themselves out of it, into the still waters of truth, justice, uprightness, peace, and holiness. The nations have hitherto been some as wolves, some as foxes, some as tigers, and some as dogs; but hereafter they shall live not as the brutes, but as God designed them to live while upon earth—living righteously in His sight. But first, oh ye nations, diligently set to work, and acquaint yourselves with that foundation of all true happiness, a right knowledge of the spirit of the Holy Scriptures. This little book will assist you in their interpretation, and having, as it were mastered the alphabet, knowledge how to govern yourselves aright will be set before you. Your eyes, oh ye nations, for a time will be averted from this little book; but some souls, and your children, will esteem it differently to yourselves, and it will be their guide. It will be like sound seed sown in fertile ground, springing up, growing apace, bearing plenteous and goodly fruit for ever!

END OF PART V.

www.ingramcontent.com/pod-product-compliance
Lightning Source LLC
Chambersburg PA
CBHW021404230426
43666CB00006B/635